GW00480470

Somerset's 50 mile Parrett Trail

by Dot Walford

**A Layperson's Guide
to its Landscapes
and its History**

Copyright © Dot Walford 2020 All Rights Reserved
The rights of Dot Walford to be identified as the author of this work
have been asserted by her in accordance with the
Copyright Designs and Patent Act 1988.

ISBN 978-1-5272-7956-8

Published in 2021 by West Country Walking Trails
16 Abbey Close, Curry Rivel, Langport, Somerset TA10 0EL
Email: dmwobbly@btinternet.com

Printed by Direct Offset, 27c High Street, Glastonbury BA6 9DR
Email: printing@directoffset.co.uk   Tel: 01458 831417

No part of this publication may be reproduced, stored in a retrieval
system or transmitted in any form or by any means electronic,
mechanical, photocopying, recording or otherwise without the prior
permission of West Country Walking Trails.

For my husband Colin

Acknowledgements

My thanks go to my friends and family who have given me so much support whilst I've been writing, helping with information, photography, proof reading, and very constructive suggestions and ideas:

Helen, Chris and Claire Walford
Dr Geoff Townson, C.Geol. FGS.
Steph Taylor
Julia Harvey
Pam O'Donnell
Doreen St John-Rushton
Patrick and Liz Rendell
Nina Ayres.

Rowena and Bill Wallace, who have helped me prepare the book. I am so appreciative for all the work they've done toward it becoming a reality.

Minnie Askey, Roger Bastable and India Thomas all of Haselbury Mill

Marcus Bishop and Scott Huntley of Waterstones, Yeovil

and Saul and Eva Harvey of Harvey's Quarry at Ham Hill.

It has been a joy to write this little book, a joy which has been increased by the help and support given by you all. Thank you.

Dot Walford
November 2020

Introduction

My little book is written as though I'm actually taking you with me along the 50 mile Parrett Trail. However, it is not intended as a guide book, although there are details of the route on geological maps, plus grid references of places visited en route to the rear of the book.

Hopefully my jottings will encourage you to pick out the parts you'd most like to see, or even better to walk the whole 50 miles.

There are pubs and cafés in most villages to help you plan your days. Maybe you could read the book as a story, or, it could be a book to take with you, enabling you to read it before walking each section. It would then give you an idea of what there is to discover each day. Whichever you do, hopefully all will be of interest and provide you with a flavour of this part of sunny Somerset.

I'm not a geologist by training but have spent many years walking the Parrett Trail, some as a guide, and have developed a deep interest in the geology, flora and fauna and the history of the area. I hope these notes will entice you to look at the countryside in a new way, to look further than just the views, pasturelands and buildings to see land formations and how they affect the way we live.

Maybe you'll feel inspired to explore more of Somerset, the land of the *Sumorsaete* – the Summer Settlers – and the county I live in and love.

There's so much to discover!

Chedington to Merriott

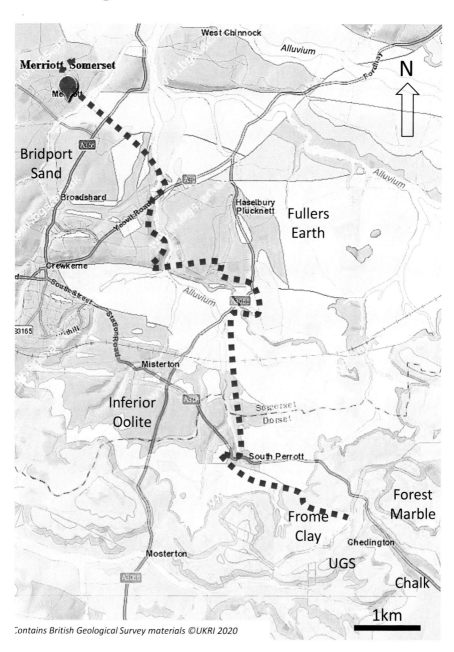

Contains British Geological Survey materials ©UKRI 2020

Chapter 1
Chedington to Merriott 10.5k (6.55mls)

Have you ever thought about why plants grow in particular areas? Have you ever wondered why stone differs in colours from region to region? Red Devon sandstone, grey and pink granite on Dartmoor and, in Somerset, a whole range of sedimentary rocks: clay/shale, sandstone and limestones of varying make-up and colours. Willows grow well on the Somerset levels and moors, with oak and ash preferring lush green pastureland.

Industries also vary from place to place. Why is this?

It is purely and simply our underlying geology which, as lay people, many of us call soil, stone and rocks!

Our journey starts at Chedington in Dorset which lies on a spur of chalk and Upper Greensand deposited as sand and lime mud on the seabed 85–100 million years ago. We're here because we meet the source of the River Parrett. On the other side of the ridge lies the source of the River Axe. The former flows northwards and the latter, south westerly. The woodland above and behind you – its floor in springtime covered with a mass of

The source of the Parrett at Chedington

bluebells – is all fed by the fertile Upper Greensand, which gained its name from small grains of dark green glauconite, which oxidise to an ochre colour when exposed to the air. Close by and amongst the woodland, standing proudly at a height of 600 ft., is a 2nd World War Memorial to the 43rd Wessex Division Territorial Army built to honour those men who perished in Normandy, July 1944.

Chedington itself is most probably named after an Anglo-Saxon called Cedda. The nearby Manor is of Norman origin and has the most wonderful views, views that we'll be able to share as we begin our trek through lush green pastureland feeding both cattle and sheep. Initially we'll encounter a rather boggy area of reeds considered to be the Parrett's source, an area to remember when we achieve our goal at Stert Point, 50 miles away. As we walk the area has now changed to Frome Clay, a marly soil. A geologist would describe these soils as 'calcareous argillaceous (sedimentary) mudstone', its fertility so evident here in this beautiful pastureland and further emphasised by oaks loving heavy clays, making it their home too, rather than the lighter and sandier Upper Greensand soils loved by the beeches we've left behind.

The contact between the Middle Jurassic Frome Clay and the overlying Mid Cretaceous Upper Greensand (65–70 million-year gap) is a springline creating a developing water course, here as the source of our Parrett companion as we descend to the delightful village of South Perrott, which brings us to yet another rock formation. You'd be forgiven for thinking that many of the houses here are built of Hamstone as they're so similar in colour to that stone. They are in fact constructed of Sherborne Stone, a Middle Jurassic Inferior Oolite (inferior as it lies beneath Great Oolite), which contains many well-preserved fossils, particularly ammonites. The rock is created by small fish-egg shaped sediment grains known as ooids, which formed in warm subtropical seas where gentle currents rolled the ooids around successively coating them in lime. Whatever the stone, the houses portray a quintessential English village.

In the midst of a cluster of houses alongside a quiet lane you'll see Pattens Cottage, formerly Court Farm. This suggests that in the vicinity the ancient Saxon Court Leet would have met to record manorial problems such as blocked ditches, obstructed paths, plus courses altered by parishioners! Ahead is the church, its origins Norman. Behind it lies the site of Mohun Castle which during 1644 provided a bed for Charles I. The only evidence today of the castle are the banks and ditches of the moat which surrounded it.

As we approach the once-turnpiked road, take time to stop at the bridge over the Parrett to look at the sculpting relevant to the water and the countryside. This was created by Evie Bodie whose work you'll see again later. To your left is Hunters Hatch, a purposely adapted thatched house, thought to have sheltered fugitives escaping from the Monmouth Rebellion. To your right and quite possibly important, is the welcoming sight of the Coach and Horses pub, just the place to quench your thirst with a welcoming pint.

Onward now into Pipplepen Lane to cross the county boundary between Dorset and Somerset. South Perrott is left behind as we enter the parish of North Perrott to discover Pipplepen Farm. What a fascinating name! Where did it come from and where did Perrott come from too? Let's start with Pipplepen.

During the 13th century, records show that a manor called Pupelpenne or Pipplepen had been created here with a large mansion, the home of the De Pipplepens built, within a moated area which we'll see later.

Pipplepen Farm is Grade II listed and dates from the 1600s. There are suggestions that some areas of the building were constructed during the 1300s, which would tally with the dating of the moated house. It is considered that the stone here is Hamstone coursed rubble with ashlar quoins and dressings. I've always considered rubble as inferior, but it is an accepted term for stone which is not dressed. Ashlar is dressed, and has squared edges plus smoothed faces.

Throughout this area, we're moving in and out of Inferior Oolite we met earlier and Fullers Earth, which I'll explain later as we approach Merriott. But we are still walking through lands used for both arable and pastureland. Again, it's the nutrients in the soil feeding them. An important one is lime.

Crossing the London South West railway line, off to our right was a onetime mediaeval deer park, and just beyond us and to our left, a wooded area containing the moat I mentioned earlier. This encloses an area raised above the surrounding ground level on which stood the 13th century mansion of the De Pipplepens.

And now we reach another quintessential English village, North Perrott, with an equally quintessential English Pub! So, who's for a pint at the Manor Arms?

Now to the village name. 1066 and all that! This was when we saw and felt the actions of William the Conqueror replacing the Saxon lords and landowners with his own French Knights, here at North Perrott, Edward de Peret. Is it reasonable then, to consider that the name Perrott originates from Peret? Is it this, or is the name derived from the river Parrett as some consider it to be?

North Perrott over the centuries has remained mainly agricultural due again to the fertility of the soils. Back to the future though, we discover an alternative industry, the birthplace during the 20th century of the Ariel Atom, a sporty, racing-type car. No roof, no doors and no windows. What fun it would be to drive!

St Martin's church, a sister to St Mary's at South Perrott, is again of Norman origin. Outside, the graveyard in spring is carpeted by snowdrops and winter aconites. It is simply beautiful. However, the graveyard also holds a mysterious, bygone tragedy! This, I think, is for you to discover!

A change of scenery now as we enter the parklands of North Perrott Manor. One of the first mature trees you'll see is the sweet chestnut. Take time to look at its bark. See the way it swirls around the trunk, as a lady's long, full skirt would swirl whilst she danced. The trees are not only beautiful to the eye, but useful too. Pastime uses have included medicinal aids with the nuts ground and used for bread making. As a mature tree the sweet chestnut is an alternative to oak – it grows faster, is tougher and easier to manipulate and craft.

At the far end of the park, we'll see North Perrott Manor built of Hamstone ashlar and Grade II* listed, as are many houses within the village. Retracing your steps and turning left as though you were leaving the pub, you'd reach the Old Teachers house c. 1800s. If though, you turned right, you'd see the picturesque Manor Farm House c.1600s. Both houses are Grade II listed and both built of Hamstone roughly squared stone with ashlar dressings.

With all this Hamstone around you, at the end of the second leg of this journey, think how exciting it will be for us all, and that includes me, to see this beautiful, honey coloured stone in situ.

Back now to the Manor House constructed during the late 1800s as a home for the Hoskyn family, the then Lords of the Manor. As with so many large estates and houses during the 2nd World War, it became home to American soldiers. Today it's an independent school which it has remained since 1949.

Moving on, we are again in an area of Inferior Oolite having left the Fullers Earth behind us. Here alongside North Perrott Orchards is evidence of how well crops respond to this limestone formation, created in part by fossilised sea shells composed of calcium carbonate.

Recognising the suitability of the soils here by the then Lord of the Manor, these orchards were set up between the two World Wars to give employment to those in need. Today on a lesser scale they are still run by a present-day member of the Hoskyn family.

Leaving the orchards behind us you'll walk a short distance between hedges of laurel which, at their end, bend and meet in an arched formation to frame the distant tower of St Bartholomew's church at Crewkerne.

To follow this comes one of my favourite spots of the trail – peaceful and scenic and full of wild flowers. Alder trees, once used for clog-making line the river banks. During the seasons there is a host of different plants: comfrey, which provides nitrogen, and in the little pond – king cups which hung in doorways in May and

Alder trees in winter

kept the witches at bay! The tiny lady's smock grows here too, its edible basal leaves tasting like watercress.

Close by are the ruins of an old grist mill, its wheel pit today home to sycamore trees. The waterwheel was fed by a leat (man-made water channel) and still to be seen flowing from the Parrett beyond.

Before we walk on, take stock of the width of the river and how it has grown from its source approximately five miles away. You'll be amazed to see how much wider it is and will continue to be until we reach our journey's end at Stert Point, approximately 45 miles beyond us. There the expanse of the river and the view as it meets the sea, is simply breath-taking.

Continuing our walk alongside the Parrett we may, if we're lucky, see herons circling above in their gentle and languid flight. Himalayan balsam, also known as poor man's orchid, lines the river banks and in amongst the reeds can sometimes be found ragged robin.

Common Teasel

There are also the common teasels, again a medicinal plant. We'll discover its other uses plus another family member later. On the opposite side of the river are the remains of brickwork associated with another leat, its flowing waters providing power to the mill wheel ahead. But for me the best is still to come: the most beautiful, circular culvert constructed from Hamstone, built to take the waters from the leat to the mill beyond, plus carrying the newly-formed turnpiked road above. The original Trail's path took you through the culvert, which enabled you to see the skills and superb craftmanship of the masons who built it. You would have stepped over giant slabs of Hamstone displaying the words, 'Where Water Once Flowed.' Sad to say, owing to land disagreements, the route has now been diverted to cross the extremely fast and busy A30, *so great care is needed here*.

Once across the road you'll enter a beautiful spot which houses holiday shepherds' huts set between the river and the leat. Nearby is an ancient packhorse bridge thought to date from the 1400s. This, until c.1830, was the original route of the turnpike road, all part of the Crewkerne Turnpike Trust.

Ahead lies Haselbury Mill surrounded by beautiful grounds where you'll also see an apparently old tithe barn – but all is not what it seems! Built recently (c.2000), using Hamstone, it's an achievement of which the talented crafts people should be proud, proud to have all played their part.

The Mill mentioned in The Domesday Book as a corn mill continued to be used as such until it closed during 1985. It has since become an hotel, plus a fantastic venue for hosting weddings. A wonderful site too for a pub lunch and maybe another pint?

Haselbury Mill Tithe Barn, c.2000, on a misty morning

Leaving the mill to your right and above us is what was once a small family farm. Today Rushy Wood Farm has become a huge dairy complex which supplies both milk and award-winning cheeses nationwide. Why is this? Nutrient-rich soils again, creating superb pasturelands for both dairy and arable.

Ahead of you are hills surrounding West Chinnock. If there's good visibility you should be able to pick out what appear to be terraces. These are in fact Strip Lynchets (bench formation), remains of the old mediaeval Field Strip System, where each man had his own three strips of land but not necessarily three side by side.

The nearby bridge crossing the Parrett was constructed c.2000 using West Country timbers with funding raised by the children of Haselbury School.

Following is the crossing of the A356 to reach Tayles Lane. Here we'll discover Tayles corn mill which, during later times converted to become a flax mill. As with so many mills the products processed changed as the economic climate dictated. Here at Tayles Mill, named after its 13th century owner, it was the same as elsewhere. Demand for flax and hemp to create linen, sailcloth and rope for the Navy was high during the 1800s, owing to the onset of the Napoleonic and Crimean wars. This was a time when Crewkerne and its surrounding merchants became wealthy men. When we reach Ham Hill, we'll discover how many of them chose to spend their wealth.

Why did the mills in this region decide to change to the processing of flax? Apart from the country's need for sailcloth and rope, what was the underlying reason which enabled this to happen?

We're back again to the geology and the soils, and here you're in an area of Fullers Earth conducive to the growing of flax and hemp. Fullers Earth, which is sandy and loamy, is composed of a variety of clay minerals but locally, particularly at Chedington, both montmorillonite and bentonite are present, together creating a de-greasing agent so important to the cloth-making process. During olden times, before the use of this agent, huge vats of stale urine were used to eliminate the grease, with the cloth being trampled by men, women and children, all made redundant by the introduction of the mechanical pummelling stocks of converted mills.

Merriott Lock Up door and window

And next, just what is this small and definitely sturdy building built using Hamstone ashlar for both walls and roof tiles? It is a Lock Up. The door has above it a small slit acting as a window, the only opening to let light and air enter. The studded door has an iron plate inner which is clad on both sides with oak facings. What was it used for? An overnight prison, housing petty offenders such as drunks and vagrants who, on the following morning, would have been brought before the local magistrate. Later, we'll be able to see a rather more upmarket Lock Up, so I'll give a little more detail then.

And now our final building, but this is one which invites you in to celebrate your day's walk. The Kings Head pub!

Whilst supping our pints at the end of our day, think about the landscapes we've walked through and experienced, and realise that they are the results of our underlying geology. It will hopefully help us to understand that our farming, both pasture and arable, and our industries – wool, linen, sailcloth and rope – are all driven by the soils over which we've walked. We eat the crops, we drink the milk, we wear the clothes made from wool and linen.

We are the product of geology!

Chapter 2
Merriott to Ham Hill 10k (6.25mls)

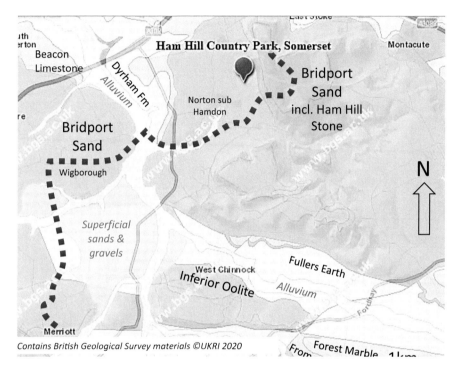

Contains British Geological Survey materials ©UKRI 2020

What's in a name? What is the origin of Merriott? The Domesday Book (1086) records the village as *Meriet* after the family of Harding de Meriet, landholder for Robert of Mortain the half-brother of William the Conqueror. The vernacular today is Mert!

The King's Head pub is thought to date from the mid-1600s, most definitely by 1685 if the story that's told is correct, that supporters of Monmouth's Rebellion plotted here. Later the pub changed its function as a plotters' den to that of a local court. Were the occupants of the Lock Up tried here?

On the first leg of our journey we walked in areas of Upper Greensand,

Frome Clay, Inferior Oolite and Fullers Earth. Today we'll be discovering Bridport Sands and alluvium, along with superficial sands and gravels. Even more geological formations will be revealed as we continue our journey towards the sea.

The Bridport Sand Formation is a modern blanket term for the Midford Sands (Bath area), Yeovil Sands and the Bridport Sands. It comprises of a fine-grained yellow-brown silt, sand, friable sandstone and sandy limestone of Lower Jurassic (Lias) age, laid down some 173–176 million years ago (the older deposits lie in the north and the younger to the south).

Here by the pub we're in an area of Bridport Sand which is succeeded by Fullers Earth. Both soils are very fertile. Way back during the 1300s, monks associated with Muchelney Abbey used these nutrient-rich soils to create a Tree Nursery here, to be followed 500 years later by Scott's Nurseries who specialised in roses and, overtime gained Royal Acclaim.

Maybe, as we are walking today in these nutrient-rich soils for quite a distance, I should mention the lucrative wool trade of the West Country. This utilised these soils to nurture good pastureland and in turn fed thousands of sheep, producing a massive amount of wool. Money poured into the country, to the church and the landowners. Day four of our route will reveal how some of those wool monies were spent.

Crossing a bridleway, note the variety of plants and trees: hedge maple its wood used to create violins and harps, elderberry, its fruit good for wine, hawthorn used as an alternative to stone walls as it grows quickly and is less costly and, stinging nettles known as the Devil's plaything.

Hart's Tongue fern

Harts tongue fern is humorously named mother-in-laws-tongue due to the length and shape of its leaves – it was also thought to cure liver diseases. All around you is your medicine cupboard and all for free! With so many edible plants around us too, it is also your larder.

Into the open fields and in sight is Ham Hill War Memorial at the end of today's walk. We cross the

Lopen Brook situated in an area of alluvium and superficial sands and gravels. We will meet these deposits again as we approach the sea beyond Bridgwater, so I'll explain more then. Very close to the brook is a pond surrounded by willows – an ideal place to see dragon flies and the smaller, to me, much more beautiful damselflies, particularly the banded blue demoiselle.

The next community we meet is Lower Stratton. According to the Oxford Dictionary of English Place-Names, "Stratton usually means 'farmstead or village on a Roman road." After the Romans this area became a Saxon estate: street in Anglo Saxon language was what we today call Old English, straét.

Let's think about the Roman occupation (43–410AD), when Somerset contained many Roman roads both major and minor. To the north of Lower Stratton approximately a mile away is the Roman Fosse Way, a major route of some 230 miles from Lincoln to Exeter. Four miles to the south west at Dinnington are the remains of a large villa containing the most beautiful mosaic floor depicting Daphne and Apollo. Television's Time Team excavated here during 2002 and again during 2006. Added to this find is the discovery of another mosaic on the outskirts of Lopen village about two miles to the south west.

If the Roman era is of interest to you, Somerset as a county should well and truly feed your needs. Later and en route is Bridgwater Museum which houses Roman remains from around its area, including Combwich a past coastal port which we visit toward the end of our trek.

Here at Lower Stratton there are two walk options: one, ours to Ham Hill, the other via South Petherton and East Lambrook and its brook where the two routes link.

Turning right, we'll walk via a narrow lane bounded by Hamstone cottages. Within their midst is the Old Forge which has mullioned windows and walls strengthened by the use of reinforcing bars. Take time to look at their decorative ends on the outside walls of the cottage. Rather than the simple and usual plain X-formation used on most houses, the blacksmith here has indulged in a little luxury. An important man in his village, he would certainly have earned his crust and I feel earned a very justifiable reward for his embellishment.

Wigborough Manor House at the end of the lane was built on the site of a Saxon estate. The original house may date from around the 1300s. The present house contains a bracket dated 1585, with another room housing an early 17th century fireplace sporting the arms of Hele of Flete. All these point to the house construction dating to the late 16th to early 17th centuries. Beyond and from the memorial stone to the Vaux family, take time to look back at the house which helps to confirm its date as its design is so obviously Tudor.

It's also worth seeing how far we've travelled since the start of the Trail, as from here the Dorset hills are in sight. Take note too of the lush green pastureland and remember why it is so and why the cattle, sheep and horses graze here – it's the bedrock of Bridport Sands.

And now let's meet a rather grown-up River Parrett. It had grown substantially when we met it after we left North Perrott but here, as we're approaching Norton-sub-Hamdon it has grown even more. It makes me think of the saying 'mighty oaks from little acorns grow' and, in a sense, that's how it is here with the River Parrett. So very exciting!

Creedy Bridge sits in an area of alluvium and is where we say goodbye to the Parrett for a while to be met by one of its tributaries, the Coleford Brook, encountering the Bridport Sand Formation once more.

Take note here of the mixed woodland above us, the first we've encountered since leaving Chedington. Ash, very partial to limestone, has been used to construct cart shafts and frames and wooden wheel rims.

Spars and liggers for thatching use were created from hazel, which brings to mind the Neolithic folk, whom we'll meet very shortly. Not in person I may add! Hazel nuts would have been part of their staple diet.

Oaks were used for their tanning properties in the leather trade, an important industry in this and surrounding areas. Glove-making from leather was a massive cottage industry which continued well into the latter part of the 1900s. Pittard's of Yeovil, a well-established family firm continues to manufacture gloves to this day. Over the years they've gained a good reputation world-wide for their quality gloves.

Maybe at this point we should again ask ourselves why these trees grow here. Why here, but not around Combwich and beyond where you'll see that trees are a rarity. It's the calcium-rich Bridport Sands again.

Walking toward Norton-sub-Hamdon alongside the brook one can take a peep at beautiful gardens nearby. As you reach Brook Street turn to the left to see within the front wall of the house, a

Hamstone Trefoil

Hamstone trefoil, beautifully sculpted by a talented mason. It is rather a surprise to find it here as most of us associate these sculptures with monastic buildings. Hamstone at its best!

Retracing your steps along Brook Street you'll see Brook House (Grade II listed). Take note of the angled gateway purposely built this way to enable easier access for carts delivering stone from Ham Hill, to the stone yard that lay behind the property.

Next is yet another village pub, the Lord Nelson. This is an 18th century Grade II listed building, originally thatched. A tell-tale sign indicating this is to look around the base of the chimneys where they meet the roof. Here very often is a cement or lead collar preventing water seeping into the attic. Another is the water tabling at both ends of the building and above the gable end of the building, which stands above any later tiled or slated roof. An obvious pointer is the steep pitch of a thatched roof. Low pitched roofs only became possible when using Welsh Slate which was readily available from the early part of the 19th century.

The church of St Mary's is Grade II listed and again Hamstone ashlar. The wrought iron pulpit and screen within have tenuous connections to Thomas Hardy, the celebrated Dorset novelist and poet. Look around the building to discover masons' marks carved into the stonework, amongst them those of William of Norton. Obviously a very talented craftsman, he left his marks elsewhere, e.g. Wells Cathedral, Beaumaris and Caernarfon castles – whilst travelling to these places no doubt transporting cartloads of Ham-

Dovecote/pigeon house, Norton sub Hamdon

stone to each venue. Close by is the listed dovecote/pigeon house, its date unknown.

This picturesque village set in such beautiful countryside is one to spend time – wandering around its streets to view the numerous magnificent houses and cottages, many listed and all constructed from the stone quarried from Ham Hill above. Eminent people have made this place home: John Constable chose to stay here and, much later, the well-known politician, Lord Paddy Ashdown lived here too.

Leaving the village, look out for the Millennium boundary stone between Norton sub Hamdon and Little Norton. This depicts stone masons and their tools.

The words quintessential village spring to mind again when we reach Little Norton. Here there are yet more delightful Hamstone houses to view, plus a picturesque old mill set amidst them – an idyllic position. The mill today offers accommodation, so why not stay for a couple of nights and soak up the atmosphere of Somerset's wonderfully diverse landscapes, its churches, pubs, bygone ports and people.

The Grade II listed mill building dates from 1782 and is very well preserved. The machinery is basically intact and is representative of a late 18th century layout, with some elements replaced in cast iron during the 19th century. After the building and machinery were restored in the 1990s it became fully operational again, having ceased commercial work during 1919. The waterwheel is overshot and fed from springs within the woodlands above. Mentioned in the Domesday Book, there has been a mill here since Saxon times.

We're now going to leave the lush pasturelands and old houses, watching the Parrett grow in width, and the level footpaths and roads. We're in for a new experience, a steep, steep climb, but it's worth it as there are panoramic views when we reach the top.

Ham Hill here we come!

Chapter 3
Ham Hill

Ham Hill sedimentary stone

Ham Hill Iron Age Fort is a very important site and part of the second leg of the Parrett Trail, but it is also and more importantly, an area with ties to so many of the places along our route. Think back to the houses we've already seen built of this unique Hamstone. It has been used far and wide over the centuries throughout Britain. Remember William of Norton, the mason who travelled to Beaumaris and Caernarfon castles, who transported and used Hamstone there? Other buildings using this stone are St David's Cathedral in Pembrokeshire, Hadrian's Wall and, closer to home, Wells Cathedral.

Harvey's Quarry, Ham Hill

Over the next few pages, I'd like to mention the peoples who have occupied this fort. I'd like to explain why Hamstone has become so sought after. Where did people source the finances to purchase the stone? What were and still are the industries created around it? It's an exciting as well as a beautiful area where it's so easy to spend a day meandering through its numerous acres.

At the start of the Trail we stood at a height of 600 ft above sea level, descending to South Perrott below at approximately 200 ft. With little variation in levels en route, here at Little Norton things are about to change. We are going to climb!

We are going to climb the ramparts of the Iron Age Fort leading to Ham Hill – a height of approximately 400ft. Climbing takes you through woodland where holly grows, a white, hard wood which in the days of carriages was used for creating whips. Sycamore, ash, oak, field maple, hawthorn and hazels as I've already mentioned, providing nuts for the Neolithic folk but also used to create hazel wands – thought to have healing properties.

A little about the ramparts: these were developed during the Iron Age (750 BC to 43 AD) as a defensive structure to the fort above. At their top and around its perimeter the fort had a wooden palisade (see information panel near the pub). Enemies attempting to capture the fort would have experienced the climb you've just made, but would have been rained on by catapults and sling shots from above – no doubt, other trajectories too!

The fort was occupied during the Iron Age by the Celtic Durotrigan tribe, its central power site here at Ham Hill which developed into a busy and important place. This prominent landmark with its massive banks and ditches must have looked not only daunting and awesome, but powerful too from the low-lying lands below.

Ham Hill around the northern spur, where the War Memorial is located, was probably the most important area of the overall fort. Trading here with peoples of the surrounding areas indicates this as being a time of prosperity. Both Iron Age currency bars along with animal bones of both cattle and sheep the latter used as food and for trade have been discovered here. Past investigations revealed a planned network of huts, fields used for cultivation and trackways linking clusters of thatched roundhouses (see info board near Stroud's Meadow). Water would have been drawn from a spring in an area known today as the Combe. Trees were felled and used for fuel and building so the fort at that time must have appeared barren, so very different from the one we see today.

Having arrived at the top of the ramparts we're now walking part of the twenty-eight-mile Liberty Trail. This begins here on the hill and finishes at Lyme Regis, its route passing through villages and towns where the Duke of Monmouth gained supporters for his rebellion against his father Charles II. During a later part of your route, you'll be able to visit the site where the Royalists and Monmouth's rebels met for their ensuing Battle of Sedgemoor during 1685, the last battle to be fought on English soil.

Reaching Norton Hill car park, we'll see the first of many magnificent views. In the valley below is Norton-sub-Hamdon and its magnificent church tower. Covering a massive area nearby are soft fruit orchards. The conical hill close to the village of Chiselborough, due south from here, appears man-made but no, it's a quirk of nature.

And now we're back to industry, lime burning. Nearby are the partial remains of a disused limekiln. Lime-burning throughout Somerset and Dorset was a massive industry during the 18th and 19th centuries. Lime had been burned during prehistoric times, the Roman era to create their valued mortar and, later for the churches and brick houses built during the 14th to 15th centuries. But boom time came with the Agricultural Revolution. Lime once again the result of the underlying bedrock, was of prime importance as a fertilizer. Transportation of lime was the beginning of the canal era, as haulage costs were much lower by this method than by pack horses.

Time to remember the areas we've walked through: lush pastureland for farming, areas where flax and hemp were grown for manufacturing rope and linens, apple orchards to feed communities – all of them making use of the nutrients of the rock formations.

Passing the Rangers' Hut, we'll set off toward the War Memorial. To our right are spoil heaps covered with wild flowers; scabious used to heal skin infections, wild parsnip which can cause skin irritation. The latter is a member of the cow parsley family, the Umbelliferae. To remember this name, think of the shape of their heads, many of them resembling umbrellas. To our left and to the north-west in the valley below can be seen the Parrett Works' magnificent Italianate chimney. Beyond is the 100ft Hamstone tower of St Martin's church at Kingsbury Episcopi, both places we'll visit on the third leg of our journey.

The War Memorial, approximately 25 ft (8m) tall, stands at the tip of the northern spur of Ham Hill, honouring the men of the Great War, World War II and the Northern Ireland conflicts.

Standing here will give you a commanding view of the surrounding landscapes. The views on a clear day are stupendous: to the north west are the Quantock Hills (Devonian age rocks) with nearby Bridgwater to their east where hopefully you'll see the spire of St Mary's church, built from the very stone that's quarried here. To the north north east are the Mendips (Carboniferous Limestone), and then east north east is the National Trust property Stourhead House. Close by and visible on a clear day is Alfred's Tower, erected to mark the spot where King Alfred allegedly defeated the Danes. It also marks the spot where the 28 mile Leland Trail begins which, if you do decide to walk the route, will eventually lead you to this magnificent viewpoint.

Let us now think of past times and the prehistoric peoples who occupied Ham Hill. There is evidence of Stone Age men, women and children living here. Tools discovered from this era have been quern stones, slingstones and pottery. And then came the Bronze and Iron Age families. Discoveries over the years of these eras have included a Belgic cremation urn containing a bronze mounted dagger, also the Iron Age currency bars I mentioned earlier. Think of how an Iron Age man might have felt when he stood at his hut door, keeping a watchful eye for approaching marauders. Think of how far we are able to see, which emphasises the importance of Ham Hill as a defensive fort. A defensive site for the Romans too. Roman finds include scale armour, coins and crocks but imagine discovering the site of a twelve-roomed Roman Villa complete with mosaic floors. Try to imagine too, the joy, the excitement a school-boy felt during the early 21st century when he discovered a Roman brooch here – wow!

Next is what I would call a 'moonscape', an area extensively quarried and, in past times quarried by hand. Quarrying continues to this day but now with the use of machinery.

This flat area is interspersed by Victorian spoil heaps (see info panel). To-day these are covered with wild flowers: buddleia, wild thyme, birds foot trefoil, great mullein and agrimony. The hill is also home to a mass of scabious and vetch. Both had definite uses: scabious (mentioned before) to cure skin infections and vetch, used to flavour Scotch Whisky. All around this area and over much of the hill the land is covered by calcareous grasslands enriched by the high calcium content within the soils. Amongst them you might be lucky to spot a pyramidal orchid or two.

Visit Dartmoor, visit the Scottish Islands and you'll see many stone rows and circles. Did you expect to see them here too? Well here they are, but not Neolithic. These were erected during the early 2000s over a 4–5year period whenever a suitable stone

Ham Hill War Memorial and standing stones

was quarried. The circle has now been linked to the Millennium as a tribute to masons who plied their trade here over many centuries.

Whilst we're in this vast area of quarrying (old and new) it seems a good time to stop and discover why Hamstone is so very important. It is a local limestone at the top of the Bridport Sand Formation, the Hamstone up to 90 ft thick. Both were deposited during the Jurassic era and both are considered to be during the Lower Jurassic some 174 million years ago. The Bridport Sands (few fossils preserved) lie beneath this band of Hamstone. The latter is a shelly limestone known as bioclastic, as it is composed of a mass of broken fossil sea shells. Because of its geological importance about 30 acres are designated as a Site of Special Scientific Interest (SSSI).

These formations were laid down when the area was covered by a warm shallow sea, in which the layers of material, both living (shells) and non-living (quartz sand), accumulated. Subsequently, these sedimentary layers became compressed with the weight of the younger Jurassic and Creta-ceous strata which once covered this area.

Hamstone is regarded as fairly soft rock and described as a 'freestone'. Be-ing fine grained, it is a rock that can be cut in any direction and is superb for all but the most delicate carving which is limited to little more than the size of a large postage stamp, as finding stone which doesn't contain pockets of clay or iron can be difficult.

If we think of the Dissolution of the Monasteries (1536–1539) with the monasteries and their lands being taken by Henry VIII, what happened to all the lands? Who benefited? Henry's closest inner circle. These men became well-to-do landowners, and, so being, purchased Hamstone to build them-selves appropriately grand homes such as Montacute, Dillington House, Barrington and many more. This was post-Roman boom time number one. Boom number two coincided with the Napoleonic Wars (1799–1815)

On the first leg of our journey we viewed Tayles Mill, a flax mill processing flax and hemp ready to be made into sailcloth and rope. Who used these? – the Navy. Who sold them to the Navy? Merchants from Crewkerne and surrounding areas who manufactured the goods and became wealthy men. How did they spend their wealth? Purchasing Hamstone to build themselves grand and impressive houses in and around Crewkerne. Visit the town today and you'll see some of these Georgian Hamstone houses which emphasise the prosperity of the town at that time. Today the stone is again being used to clad new homes as well as restorations for older buildings. This in turn creates employment within the building trade by using this beautiful honey coloured stone helping to support the county's economy.

This site of extensive quarrying is now Ham Hill Country Park – a play-ground for tourists. So, as we're all tourists and before we wend our way toward the pub, we'll pass the site of the east gate of the Iron Age fort and, in the valley below, mediaeval strip lynchets. There is an information board here, its picture giving an image of how the fort may have appeared around 2000 years ago. On reaching the pub look at its sign which I'll explain when we're here at the beginning of the start of the third leg of our journey.

Why not spend a day here wandering through woodlands, discovering the site of the spring at Combe where the Neolithic folk drew their water? If it is flowers and grasses and wee animals you're most interested in, then Stroud's meadow surrounded by dry-stone walls is the place for you. Nearby are Evie Bodie's sculptures which represent a Bronze Age axe head and bucket-mount, complete with carvings detailing those found on the original bucket handle. Both were discovered here at Ham Hill.

And to end your day, what better way than mulling over what you've seen and achieved, whilst enjoying a pint at the Prince of Wales pub – I'd love it.

Evie Bodie's Timestones

Over two days we've covered thirteen miles and a variety of underlying geological formations and soils. Initially we discovered farming, fruit growing, plus rope and linen manufacturing. On our second day we've travelled mainly over Bridport Sands, interspersed by smaller areas of Fullers Earth, Alluvium, superficial sands and gravels. Industries over both days have remained much the same until we reached Norton-sub-Hamdon, where there was evidence of a previous stone-masons' yard. Approaching Ham Hill, we discovered the extensive industry of lime burning, followed at last by seeing Hamstone in situ – a building stone that's been worked by the masons for centuries and continues to be worked to this day. We've learned about the people who purchased the stone and about those who continue to do so; what it was used for and more importantly how it was financed. Today in the 21st century Ham Hill is providing another industry, tourism – why is this? Yes, there are magnificent views, woodland walks plus areas great for youngsters to scramble around. Sheep graze here amidst Victorian spoil heaps now covered with a mass of flowering plants – all of interest to visitors, but what lies below this captivating Country Park? The most important food for plant life, for our agriculture, for us – limestone.

What would we be without our amazing geology?

Ham Hill to Langport

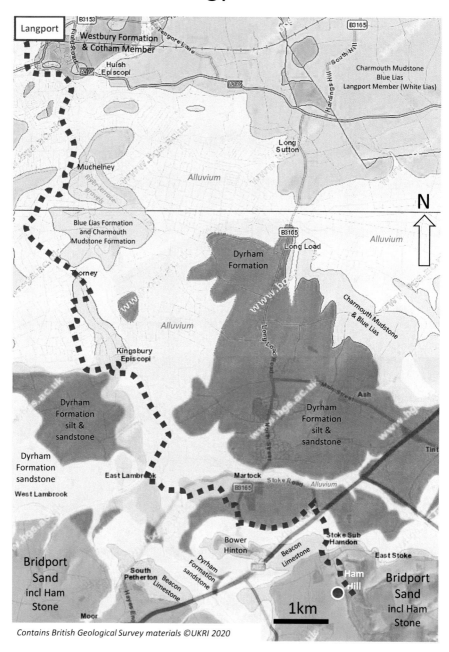

Contains British Geological Survey materials ©UKRI 2020

Chapter 4
Ham Hill to Langport 16km (10mls)

I'm starting today by mentioning royalty. Here at Ham Hill much of the site known as Duchy Land is owned by the Prince of Wales. Above us as we stand beside the pub is its sign representing the Plume of Feathers, the heraldic badge of the Prince. His motto is '*Ich Dien*' meaning 'I serve'. Later as we walk through Stoke sub Hamdon, we'll pass a cottage with both badge and motto moulded into the hoppers of the cast iron drainpipes.

We begin our journey by descending from the War Memorial. As we do, we'll hopefully be able to see (dependent on tree height), one of Somerset's Fives Walls. This one, situated in the Fleur de Lys pub car park, is built from Hamstone. On the last leg of our journey we'll be able to see another, but this time constructed of brick. Hamstone was readily available here whereas in the Bridgwater area because of the underlying bedrock there, bricks were a major industry. *Geology to the fore again!*

What are Fives Walls? Fives are thought to be linked to the old Basque game of Pelota which may have been brought to this country by prisoners taken during the Spanish wars. Here at Stoke sub Hamdon the wall is sometimes referred to as 'the Spanish Wall'. A few miles away at Hinton St George is another wall, this time of Hamstone ashlar. Discovered there was what is thought to be a Spanish gold coin, helping to substantiate the origin of these walls. How is it played? By two people in a similar way to squash, but the ball can be batted by the hand or a racket.

Approaching Stoke sub Hamdon, followed by Bower Hinton and Martock, we descend the outcrop of the Lower Jurassic Bridport Sand Formation and cross the Beacon Limestone Formation to the outcrop of the underlying sandstones of the Dyrham Formation. Nearing Bower Hinton and Martock, the Dyrham Formation becomes siltier and softer as we descend the geological sequence.

The Beacon Limestone Formation (formerly known as the Junction Bed) was deposited around 180 million years ago during the Lower Jurassic period. It is a highly fossiliferous hard, dull rusty-brown ferruginous limestone, once widely used as a building stone. There are many former quarries scattered along the outcrop.

The sandstones of the Dyrham Formation are made up of grains of sand identical in appearance with those that are churned up by waves breaking on a beach. Most grains consist of rounded quartz, but there are others made up of felspar and mica. Sandstones are formed from recycled material from older rocks such as granite, which contain the same minerals. Finally, these grains can be cemented together by calcite, a white or colourless mineral consisting of calcium carbonate. This is a major constituent of sedimentary rock such as limestone and is deposited in caves to form stalactites and stalagmites, so why not visit Cheddar Caves to see these in situ and experience a little more of Somerset.

The lower (earlier) part of the Dyrham Formation is comprised of a grey to greenish-grey silts and sandy mudstone, often interspersed with calcareous sandstone.

With the changing geological bedrock, maybe you're expecting a difference in the surrounding landscape and industries. Well no not yet; that excitement is still to come. For a little longer after we've left both Stoke sub Hamdon and Bower Hinton, we'll still be walking amidst fields of green pastureland, cattle and sheep.

We continue our walk through Stoke sub Hamdon via North Street. As well as some superb Hamstone houses there is also the old Priory, now a National Trust property. The buildings were constructed during the 1300s for the priests of the chantry chapel of St. Nicholas (now destroyed) and formerly housed in the castle complex a little farther on. Today the Priory consists of an open hall, first floor chapel, a circular dovecote that once housed 500 pigeons, and barns that were restored during the 1960s. A short distance away is Castle Farm lying close to the site of the Beauchamp family home/castle, complete then with St Nicholas' chapel. Note the nameplate of the farm; above it is a shield decorated by heraldic ermine spots, I imagine a part of the Beauchamp's family emblem. Did the Beauchamp family line their robes with rabbit fur sourced from their Ham Hill rabbit warren or, did they line them with squirrel? Only an Earl had the right to wear ermine, the latter sourced from the short-tailed stoat?

Crossing the A303 we're in an area closely connected with the Roman Fosse Way – a military road for the movement of soldiers. Later it became a busy and important turnpike road, good for transporting goods from industries such as quarried Hamstone and gloving in the surrounding areas.

Before we reach Bower Hinton and as we're in farmland, it's a good time to take stock of the plants and trees around us. In abundance are elder trees, considered in olden times to have magical properties. Planted by the house it would keep the Devil away! Beware if you burnt it as you'd then meet the Devil! Medicinally it was used as an aid for rheumatism, colds and flu and for well-being, as we discovered earlier in our walk, berries that produce superb red wine!

Hogweed is said to have been used as pig food, hence its name. Look at the flower heads' shape denoting yet another member of the Umbelliferae family.

Mistletoe is a parasite and common in the area growing on any tree with rough bark, but it's particularly fond of the apple tree. Kissing underneath the mistletoe is thought to date back to the 17th century. Why did it evolve? Who knows, but it is all part of Christmas and it is *fun!*

Hogweed and mares tail

Entering Bower Hinton, a part of the huge Manorial lands of Martock, we'll take a diversion to visit Yandles café, its woodyard, shop and craft centre; maybe to share and sample a super lunch or scrumptious tea and cake.

Today we are all aware of needing to diversify in the way we lead our lives, and how we earn our livings. Yandles has been no exception. Since its beginnings as a building company, founded during the late 1800s, diversification came during the First World War, by securing a contract to supply coffin boards to the Ministry of Defence. Yandles' wood supply was sourced from Somerset's many elm trees. The 1970s spelt disaster when Dutch Elm disease struck and as a consequence Yandles' timber source disappeared. Time to diversify again. This time the decision was made to buy timbers from around the world. Having now gained an international reputation, the company hosts an annual woodworking and craft event with people visiting from countries far and wide.

And to follow, how about a visit to Martock's All Saints Church? Built of

Hamstone during the 13th century it is now Grade 1 listed. On the outside of the building are numerous scratch dials. Inside there are 87 angels, many made of wood which adorn a beautifully carved timber roof. In the Sanctuary attached to the altar is one of the famous Thompson mice. *Do ask permission to be able to see this. It is most important that you do.*

Returning to Bower Hinton our journey continues amongst present day allotments and rows of cottages close by with long and narrow gardens. We're now discovering a developing history. Remember the strip lynchets we saw at Ham Hill? All part of the medieval field system where each man was allocated his 3 strips of land by the Lord of the Manor. Here, these long strips of land, now allotments, originate from those times. As a rough measure use your feet to assess the length and breadth of each patch. Having done this myself, you'll discover they're approximately 220 yards by 7 yards each way. Now remember the length of a furlong, 220 yards. Why was this measurement so important? In those times it was considered as being the amount of land a man could expect to plough in a day. Not the modern plough we know, but one pulled by oxen and most probably with only one plough shared between many.

Parrett Works Italianate chimney

Still walking through the fields we'll soon be able to see the tall Italianate chimney created for use by an iron foundry – all part of the Parrett Works, its design obviously mid-19th century following the fashion of those times.

The original mill here at Parrett Works is one of two mills in the area to have been mentioned in the Domesday Book. Today the buildings of both brick and Hamstone, the latter cut square, are Grade II* listed. The mill, powered by the waters of the Parrett close by, has a varied history – grinding grain, apple-crushing plus processing snuff, flax and hemp. To further the production of flax and hemp, to the rear of the buildings are the remains of a 19th century rope walk. If this is of special interest, then another day's exploration of Somerset could be a visit to discover Dawes Twine Works at West Coker, now up and running as a fully restored rope walk. As an iron foundry the one-time mill here at Parrett works produced traction engines, threshing machines, water wheels, flax and spinning machinery and more. It had also been used, as mentioned before, to produce yarn and canvas, which in time proved to be uneconomical, with the com-

Parrett Works main building

pany going into liquidation. Today the buildings are used as industrial units housing individual businesses.

Opposite the mill are workers' cottages, all Grade II listed. These in a sense bring us visually a little closer to Bridgwater and its far-reaching brick and tile industry. Their roofs here have been topped with what I call Bridgwater Angle tiles, now known as Triple Delta. As we get closer to Bridgwater, we'll see more and more of the industry's output, not only tiles, but bricks and beautifully crafted finials.

Walking by the Parrett again, its banks are home to numerous ash trees, but they are also home to Hemlock. *Beware, this plant is extremely poisonous*. It is another member of the, Umbelliferae family and for me, the one with the most attractive foliage. It grows to a height of approximately 6 ft with sturdy stems. Maroon-coloured blotches along the stems will help you to recognise this beautiful, but deadly plant.

Leaving the River Parrett, we'll now meet the East Lambrook brook, its banks lined with comfrey that we've spoken of before, its useful properties include medicinal, fertilizer for the garden and a one-time food for pigs. Last but not least there is its beauty, clusters of tubular bell-shaped flowers of blues, pinky-reds and whites. And then we're back with the Parrett again. Alongside the river is Gawbridge Mill, once a grain mill but now a very pleasant bed and breakfast venue. Yet another possible place to stay and have time to explore more of this wonderful county.

The actual bridge at Gawbridge (damaged severely during the Civil War), is considered to be the innermost point that barges from Bridgwater could navigate. On each side of the river banks are large and flat areas known as Coats Wharf. Here goods such as iron, bricks, lime and timber would have been offloaded onto either packhorses or horse and carts to continue their journey inland.

A question here! Nearby is the hamlet of Coat, a beautiful place which contains many 16th and 17th century Hamstone properties. My query is this. As they were built when the river trade was so prosperous, were they built for the well-to-do shipping merchants who plied their trade via the River Parrett? Was this the reason for the hamlet's name?

The level riverside walk to Kingsbury Episcopi from Gawbridge is delightful. En route reaching an area full of flag iris we'll see land regeneration in process. This one-time semi-circular inlet would have been a winding bay (similar to lay-bys on our roads), as the width of the river here was too narrow for barges to pass one another. But, with the decline of river trade during the early 20th century with less craft on the river, the area began to fill with silt deposits, hence the land development you see today.

Meadowsweet leaves (left) and mares tail (right)

However narrow the river was for barges, its growth has been tremendous since we started at the river's source at Chedington. It is also very languid here: tranquil too. It's an idyllic area.

A plant I'm very fond of is meadowsweet that has the same properties as willow (salicylic acid) and therefore good for aches and pains. Its name has come from its use in mead. Apparently, it was Elizabeth 1st's favourite flower, using it to conceal body odours!

As we passed the winding bay, we saw masses of flag iris also known as Jacob's sword. It is considered that it may be the origin of the French royal symbol, the 'fleur de lys'. Again, like so many plants it has useful properties, its roots used by medieval monks to make black ink. Think of those wonderful manuscripts they created and ask yourself the question, which plants were used to gain gold, pink, green, red and more.

Himalayan Balsam, a plant I've mentioned before has gained the names poor man's orchids and jumping jacks. The latter is very appropriate as the exploding seeds can travel a distance of 36 ft, hence its rapid spread. As it smothers plants around it, Wildlife Trusts hold 'Balsam Bashing' days whilst attempting to cull this beautiful plant, ranked at the top of the enemy plant list alongside the destructive Japanese Knotweed.

Another spreading plant is horse or marestail. It is also known as the Lego plant or pewterwort: Lego as the stems are made up of segments and pewterwort, as the stems are lined with crystals of silica and act as a fine sandpaper so good for scouring pots and pans. If the plant is boiled in water it can be used as a fungicide against mildew.

The Devil's plaything is yet another plant we've seen before. However, here's a little more about this rampant plant. Villages such as Nettlecombe (Dorset) and Nettlebed (Oxfordshire) are said to have been named after the plant. The stinging nettles' young leaves can be used in salads and soups. Its fibrous stems (similar to flax) and roots were used as an alternative for creating string and cloth-making owing to dwindling cotton supplies during the 1st World War. The leaves full of chlorophyll came to the fore here in Britain during the 2nd World War when they were used as a dye for camouflage nets.

If we're lucky we may see wild hops and hopefully their beautiful fruits. Hops are a member of the Cannabis family and closely related to hemp, drink and drugs! Let's stay with the hops. During Saxon times beer was known as ale and flavoured by herbs. All was about to change. With the influx of the Flemish weavers during the 14th and 15th centuries, came the introduction of using hops rather than herbs as a flavouring which produced a slightly bitter taste. This has to be, I feel, the reason for our beers now being known as bitter. A little later on our journey we'll see more evidence of the impact these Flemish people made on our lives and industries.

There's a possibility that we may see plantains. The round or broad-leaved variety can withstand any amount of harsh treatment and so it seems can the ribbed or narrow leaved variety. This little plant became common in the British Isles at a time when Stone Age man cleared the trees from great swathes of our lands approximately 10,000 years ago. There is evidence, obtained from analysis of the pollen found preserved in peat and lake sediment, that the plantain flourished widely at that time. Incidentally, the hardy birch tree (not seen in this area) also regenerated then.

Mid-summer is a time to look out for dragon and damselflies. Damselflies have a fluttering flight and a very delicate build, holding their wings vertically when resting as a butterfly does, whereas the much larger dragonfly holds its wings horizontally: its life above the water is approximately a month, having spent the previous two years underwater in the nymphal state. For me, maximum points for beauty go to the damselfly.

We're now approaching Kingsbury Episcopi. Originally named Kingsbury after the king who was the former landowner, it later came under the ownership of the Bishop of Bath and Wells. It is then that the additional name of Episcopi (Latin for Bishop) came into use.

Kingsbury Episcopi is where we'll begin to notice a change in foliage and the overall landscape. Why is this? We're back to the bedrock, our geology.

Ask yourself at this point, what lies beneath my feet?

As the geological map shows, we are now on the earliest Jurassic 'Blue Lias' – a series of grey to blue thin-bedded limestones interspersed with layers of dark organic shale, mudstone and marl. This is the time when ammonites first made an appearance and rapidly evolved throughout the Jurassic to become extinct at the end of the Cretaceous Periods.

For centuries these Blue Lias limestones have been used for tomb ledger slabs, cement-making and today as in the past, used for building blocks. However, because of the stones' thinly layered bedding it is of no use for carving. But, as we discovered whilst at Ham Hill, we now know that Hamstone is. Right in front of your very eyes is the evidence: the 100 ft high Hamstone tower of St Martin's church and nearby the carving of St Martin tossing his cloak to a beggar. This is not the only Hamstone here, the door and window dressings are too. Now take a look at the body of the church, not Hamstone but Blue Lias. Get a little closer to touch, feel and see the difference in textures, the change of colour and note the structure of both stones as they lie side by side.

St Martin has a sister church at Huish Episcopi, very close to Langport. This building constructed by a master mason, is in the main built from Blue Lias.

The story goes, and it is a story only, that the master mason constructed Huish church tower and his apprentice constructed this one at Kingsbury. When the master viewed the work of his apprentice, feeling that this work was far superior to his own, he proceeded to climb the tower at Kingsbury and threw himself to his death in utter despair.

St. Martin, Kingsbury Episcopi

During the Victorian era, much of St Martin's interior was considerably altered. The Hamstone arcades date from the 14th century and the upper medieval glass in the windows is all that remains after vandalism caused by soldiers during the Civil War (1642–1651). One piece left gives a clue to the time of its making. To the right of the chancel sits the organ and situated in the east window of this transept is a piece of stained glass, featuring a man of his time complete with a fashionably-styled haircut.

Most villages had their church close to the essential village pub and Kingsbury Episcopi is no different. The Wyndham Arms (named after a previous landowner) serves good food and real ales. One of the local ciders is from Burrow Hill. You might like to visit the brewery (a couple of miles away), to sample the ciders and discover a little about how they are made.

As we've been discovering since we began our trek, the bedrock and soils have been and are the reason why certain crops perform so well. Since we left Chedington the soils have been this nutrient-rich limestone, so when you're amongst this vast area of cider orchards think of the trees absorbing these as they grow. And then think of us being able to enjoy the fruits of their labours!

There's no getting away from it and as I've stated before, *we are the product of geology.*

On leaving the pub, having viewed the lock up close by, as we walk, the underlying bedrock is about to change the landscapes we've been walking through over the last few miles. It will be quite dramatic.

However, don't let me forget the nearby lock up or the tiny toll house a short stroll away. Do you remember the very simple lock up we saw at Merriott? I did say at the time that we'd meet a rather more upmarket one and here it is. Octagonal in shape, its walls are constructed of Hamstone ashlar blocks. The roof is covered with large Hamstone tiles, topped as they come to a point by the most beautifully sculpted ball finial, a decorative tile which usually stands upright and forms the terminal at the top of the gable end of houses. There are two small lancet windows and the door is again as it was at Merriott – an iron inner core clad on both sides by wood all studded together with iron bolts. The interior was extremely basic and contained no sanitary arrangements!

Why were they built? They were overnight prisons housing petty offenders, drunks and vagrants who were brought before the magistrates on the following day. As the parish had to cover any expenses incurred, these vagrants were moved on as quickly as possible. With a newly-formed police force in 1820 created by Robert Peel, better-equipped cells were built alongside police stations and many lock ups fell into disrepair.

One particularly interesting lock up is at Castle Cary, also known as a Round House. Maybe another Somerset visit?

The road we're standing by is a link to the above very attractive small town of Castle Cary as from 1753–1879 this was all part of the Langport, Somerton and Castle Cary Turnpike Trust. Linked again are the tiny toll houses, one just a five-minute walk away erected during the early part of the 19th century along with its twin a mile away at Muchelney.

Leaving Kingsbury, we're heading for an area which, when I first set my eyes on it, seemed to me purely and simply amazing. Gone were the ash and the oak and in came the willows. Then as it is now, these were areas of flat pastureland but all of them interspersed with reeds and sedges, many of them surrounded by wet fences. What are these and why are they so named? All will be revealed a little later.

It's a good time to look out for possible sightings of curlew, lapwing, snipe and mallard. You might be lucky to spot a crane but you'll most probably hear them as they trumpet their deep and lasting call. The bittern too now breeds on the Levels having been introduced here during the mid to late 20th century. Later once we've passed Bridgwater, we'll be discovering birds associated with coastal areas so for those of you who are keen birdwatchers this is something to look forward to.

And then of course there is the flora to see. There are sedges, marsh orchids, purple loosestrife and cuckoo flower, also known as lady's smock. Rushes are abundant too, and as we've discovered with most plants, they have their uses. Stripped of their outer skin, their inner core was then soaked in beeswax or tallow to provide a home-made and very simple candle. If using tallow, the smell must have been atrocious. The monied monks however used beeswax from their apiaries so were able to follow the law stating that all candles for church use must be made using beeswax.

Let's now stand and view this new and flat landscape. In the distance are the Blackdown Hills, another area you might enjoy exploring. You can see the Burton Pynsent Monument, locally known as the Cider Monument which stands majestically on Troy Hill. At 140 ft at the top, you'd be approximately 350–400 ft above sea level. The views over the flat moorlands from there are spectacular. The monument was designed with a Portland stone exterior (think of St Paul's cathedral) by Capability Brown for William Pitt the Elder and erected during 1767 as a tribute to Sir William Pynsent, owner of the estates on which it was built. The Burton estates were hugely affected by the government's proposal of a 10 shillings tax on a hogshead (54 gallons) of cider. 10 shillings (50p) would have paid a labourer for five days' work. Pitt strongly opposed this levy. In those times agricultural workers were paid in part cash and part a cider allowance. I think we can all understand Pynsent's concern about his forthcoming and possibly dwindling income. So great was his gratitude to Pitt that on his death, Sir William Pynsent left his entire estate to him.

Standing here amidst the moorland it's time for us to stop and think yet again. What has altered to create such a different landscape to that we've previously been walking though? We're no longer on rock formations of sandy, shelly limestones, we're on a layer of blue lias, covered by clay and then topped with peat which makes it easier to understand why the foliage has changed. Think about your own gardens: some of you are able to grow root crops, some of you are not and this you realise is that your own soils consist of different nutrients. The same has happened and is still happening here.

At Ducks Corner (why Ducks, I ask myself) we reach the village of Thorney and meet again the turnpike road we left behind us at Kingsbury Episcopi. To use the road, drovers, carts and carriages would have paid a toll for each mile they travelled, paying a different tariff for each individual form of transport. To be able to assess the costs, milestones became compulsory during the mid-18th century. Here, opposite the one-time local pub – the Rising Sun, was until the early part of the 21st century a milestone – a mile away from the Kingsbury toll house and a mile away from Muchelney's toll house ahead.

Thinking back to Gawbridge we discovered that Bridgwater barges off loaded their goods at Coats Wharf onto either pack horses* or carts to be transported inland. Some of the coal may well have come via this route to offload again here at the coalyard, the hauliers no doubt making good use of their time visiting the Rising Sun! However, with the coming of the branch railway (1853) came the demise of the turnpike roads and in later times the demise during 1966 of the railways too.

From here, you might like to take a short detour to visit Silent Mill, now owned by Evie Body the sculptress who created the Timestones at Ham Hill. Most probably there were mills on this site before this one was built during 1853, that worked as a grain mill until the 1960s. To me this is such a beautiful building, constructed of coursed and squared Blue Lias with just a few additions of Hamstone. The mill has a working iron overshot wheel with gabled housing. Alongside the weir is a half lock and beyond it the mill pond. The lock would have been used when the River Parrett was still navigated by barges, that is, of course until the railways came.

Silent Mill was the last working mill on the Parrett as it continued to flow towards the sea. Why? Downstream, the river has insufficient fall (1ft per mile) to have been used to power mills, but upstream where the river is obviously more powerful, we've seen Haselbury Mill, the Parrett Works and Gawbridge Mill: all have used this river's mighty power to drive their wheels. 'Mighty' you might query, as until now we've only seen a tranquil and peaceful waterway. But wait until later on our journey when we see this river in all its glory. It's magnificent!

Silent Mill, Thorney

We are all aware how badly this area floods so my feelings are that the above minimal fall of the river has to be a contributory factor to the length of time the waters linger on the low, flat moorlands. Here at Thorney as at Creedy Bridge near Norton sub Hamdon, we're again walking in an area of alluvial soils which only change as we approach Langport. I'll leave details of this until Chapter 5. However, we're now seeing the difference in the landscape that the change of bedrock and soils have brought. Left behind us are the extensive areas of lush green pastureland, although as we approach Muchelney there *are* areas of these, but when the winter rains descend, they can become a long-lasting seascape. At times such as these and with the late afternoon sun playing on the waters it's a spectacular sight, good for those of you who love photography, and artists too, which reminds me of the willow and its bark. Do have a closer look, particularly at the older trees, as the pattern of the bark is so beautiful and distinct. In fact, look at the patterns on all mature trees. They can stand alone as black and white photographs or a painting. Don't forget to look at the leaves, their colours and shapes plus the feel of them. The softness of beech leaves in spring I find so magical, evoking much emotion within me. But I'm waxing lyrical so let's move on to our next point of call, Midelney Pumping station, one of many on the moor.

Midelney has a twin at Langport and both have a definite 1960s style of architecture about them. Together, they help to drain the south and west

Midelney Bridge from the pumping station

moors. Originally powered by diesel they now use electricity. A little more detail about the stations will come to the fore in Chapter 5.

This is a place to share a picnic and to enjoy the views. Churches galore! Drayton with its stubby little tower, All Saints at Langport, Huish Episcopi and Muchelney too, and behind us as we face toward Langport, St Martin's at Kingsbury Episcopi. Close by is Midelney Manor, hidden by a clump of trees. A Grade I listed building constructed of brick, it includes a falconry mews dating to the 16th century. Legend has it that Midelney Manor was used by the merry monks as their summer retreat which again as legend suggests, had fishponds, vineyards and hunting dogs. Did this include wine, women and song? Certainly, the monks were admonished by the Bishop for rather too much good living! Today the manor is open to the public as a superb wedding venue.

Wildlife abounds here, swans, herons, snipe and the elusive kingfisher, the latter who made an appearance for me a few years ago when I was here with a group of walkers, several whom were experiencing this for the very first time. Here, you are now approaching the half way point of your journey. Looking back to the south are the Dorset Hills where we started, a little under twenty-five miles away. Only another twenty-five left! So much more to enjoy and discover.

Southmoor drain is a waterway which flows from the Parrett and into the lock here to continue until it meets incoming waters from the River Isle, both combining to create the water needed for the Westport Canal. The masonry lock at Midelney measures seventy feet by fourteen being constructed to accommodate the Parrett barges that were sixty feet long. The barges which carried a twenty-five-ton load (mostly coal), were manned by two men who occasionally used a small, square sail. They used horse power too, and as we near Muchelney we'll be walking along part of the old tow path. At Bridgwater you'll be able to see more evidence of horse-powered barges.

Approaching Westover Bridge and Muchelney we'll be able to see a bridge abutment, just a little that's left of the old branch railway. The line established during 1853 was constructed using broad gauge (a little over six feet

Bridge abutment at Muchelney

in width) but after twenty years the line was changed to the usual standard gauge (four feet, eight and a half inches). It began its life at Langport where it was connected to the main line, then wended its way through Thorney, Martock, Montacute and Yeovil, its final destination. Sad to say the line succumbed to Beeching's legislation and closed during the mid-1960s. A little way after Langport we'll be able to view the main line plus its spectacular viaduct.

From Westover Bridge a very short detour will take you to Muchelney Abbey, today under the guardianship of English Heritage. Benedictine monks were established here thirteen hundred years ago but their living was destroyed, most probably by the Danes. The Saxon Abbey constructed during the 10th century was again destroyed, but this time by the Normans. If you do visit, you'll be able to see the foundations of this later abbey beside buildings dating back to the 14th and 15th centuries; these are built using both Hamstone and Blue Lias.

The church of St Peter and St Paul has a 15th century tower and nave roof, plus some very interesting floor tiles in the sanctuary. Paintings on the nave roof are locally known as the 'naughty' angels and are thought to be of German origin. Whilst there, just take a tiny peek to see them! To the south of the church are the remains of a praying cross used as an area by itinerant monks to preach to the people.

Here too is the Priest's House dating back to 1308 and thought to be the oldest in the country. The house is occupied by National Trust tenants so appointments need to be made to visit the property.

Last but not least you'll be able to see Kingsbury's twin sister toll house, standing beside the same turnpike road we stood by at Kingsbury and then again at Thorney.

Priest's House, Muchelney

You might be wondering why both Thorney and Muchelney end with 'ney', which when translated means island. The overall name of Muchelney means great island, as the land on which the abbeys were built lies at twenty feet above sea level. This is slightly higher than the ten to fifteen feet of the surrounding lands.

Thorney is Old English (Anglo Saxon) for thorn tree island. I'm assuming that the island association relates to Thorney's isolation from other villages, as all areas are on much the same level.

From Huish Bridge we'll be able to see the nearby confluence of the Rivers Parrett and Yeo, the latter losing its identity to the Parrett. The source of the Yeo lies in Dorset north of Sherborne and above the parish of Poyntington, approximately fifteen miles away. We mentioned the Leland Trail when we were at Ham Hill. If you were to walk this route you'd walk beside a short stretch of the Yeo when close to Yeovilton Fleet Air Arm station and its museum. Yet another place to visit!

Here too whilst we're standing on the bridge, we're on part of an old drove way. These were created across the moors to enable cattle and sheep to be moved from place to place into fields surrounded by wet fences or rhynes to drain them. Today the rhynes are the responsibility of the Environmental Agency with the ditches cared for by the farming community.

During the 17th and 18th centuries the number of rhynes was greatly increased due to the Land Enclosure Acts. In came the large land owners who removed the previous rights of local people to rural land they had used for generations. As compensation, these displaced people were offered alternative land which cramped their usual farming ways, plus the land was usually inferior in quality, with often no access to water or wood. The upside for the large landowners was their new found ability to be able to manage and improve these newly-acquired lands which in turn created the need for more rhynes to drain them. We'll talk a little more about rhynes and their uses when we reach Burrowbridge.

I feel the following lines are so very apt!

> *They hang the man and flog the woman*
> *That steals the goose from off the common;*
> *But let the greater villain loose,*
> *That steals the common from the goose.*

However, let's return to the Parrett and Yeo. Try to imagine yourselves standing here one hundred years ago, when these rivers would have been busy with barges carrying goods to Gawbridge along the Parrett and along the Yeo to Ilchester to wharfs where in Roman times and beyond, goods would have been offloaded.

And now it's time to wonder at the beauty of the tower of St Mary's Church at Huish Episcopi. This is the one that the master mason built, but just look at the intricate lattice work pattern to the tower's top, a tower constructed of Blue Lias. Again, the window and door dressings are of Hamstone as at Kingsbury. Pop in to the south transept to take a look at the eastern window there. The stained glass of the window was designed by Burne Jones. The inner medieval roof has been repainted in the most delicate blue, thought to be the colour used during those times. This is another Wool church as was Martock, and all in good time we'll understand why.

For quite a way now we have been walking on alluvial soils, but for a very short while before we return to the as yet unexplained alluvium, we're about to enter an area of undifferentiated Charmouth mudstone and Blue Lias. The earliest Jurassic blue lias was laid down above the White Lias of the latest part of the Triassic period, the latter here being known as the Langport Member. The Triassic-Jurassic boundary is dated as 201 million years ago.

Approximately a mile to the north of Langport, White Lias is still commercially quarried. There the height above sea level is approximately two hundred and fifty feet and it is very wooded, the plants and trees obviously loving the abundant limestone nutrient. Isolated areas of this Langport Member are to be found in and around the town, but in the main it is predominantly surrounded by Charmouth mudstone and Blue Lias.

Speaking of heights, the highest point of Langport, known as The Hill is only a mere seventy feet, but the views as you stand in the graveyard of All Saints Church at its top are stupendous, revealing some of the areas you've walked over during the last few days.

Close to the church is the 13th century, Grade I listed Hanging Chapel, in an area where in Saxon times markets were held. Walking from here you'd approach Bow Street from a height which would allow you to overlook a mass of different styles of roof, with a huge range of colours. They are just amazing! The brickwork too is of interest, most of it would be of the local style but there are areas where this changes to Flemish Bond. Most of us are aware of the Flemish weavers and their skills within the lace-making industry, but they also brought their building skills creating a new style of brickwork. Why were they here? Religious persecution in the main, but many would have been traders from the Low Countries, some of whom would have integrated within the local community.

Langport's name has over the centuries changed several times. During the 10th century it was *Longport*, in the Domesday Book of 1086 it was *Lanport*, a little later it became known as Langport, considered to mean 'long market town'. If you look at the centrally-positioned Bow Street built on a series of arches, you'll understand why, as it extends from one end of the town to the other. From the 16th to the very early 20th centuries this street would have been full of carts laden with goods coming out through Great Bow Wharf that lies to the west of the town. These streets were lined with approximately 13 pubs and ale houses or more. Market Day was no doubt a merry one!

At the western end of Bow Street, you'll see houses that are leaning back toward the moorlands. They've been built on foundations of Blue Lias topped with peat. The latter constantly changes with rainfall: when dry, the peat shrinks; when wet, it swells, causing the movement of the buildings. This unstable situation helps us to understand the reason for the con-

Bow Street, Langport, from the west

struction of thirty-one firm foundation arches built to give stability to the street, possibly created by the Romans.

On both sides of the street and close to the wharf are what were originally goods yards – Baulks Yard for timber floated up the river and stored for drying, Pococks Yard for coal, Beards Yard, once an iron foundry, and Stacey's Yard where harnesses were made. Alongside these yards was the Dolphin Hotel which housed and fed bargees.

A good place to stand is on Great Bow Bridge which spans the Parrett and overlooks Great Bow wharf. Today this area has been transformed to house not only environmentally-friendly homes, but a café too, so very different from yesteryear when boats would have been off loading iron, coal, timber and most probably bricks and tiles manufactured at Bridgwater. Until 1839 goods being transported to Gawbridge would have been hand-balled off onto smaller barges to continue upstream. The bridge's nine arches were too narrow to accommodate the larger vessels, but this was about to change. With the setting up of the Parrett Navigation Company it was decided to rebuild the bridge with three larger arches, saving so much work for the river men.

The river trade here was a very lucrative industry run by the wealthy Stuckey family who opened their bank, not only here at Langport but in Bristol too. Their banknote circulation at the beginning of the 19th century was second only to that of the Bank of England. The Stuckey family were the instigators of the construction of the Westport Canal during the 1830s, built to counteract the newly-formed Chard canal from taking away their coal trade. But by the 1840s they were both superseded by the railway, and as we now know the railway was superseded by road haulage.

There is so much more to tell about this tiny town than I've done in my little book: the Battle of Langport and the prison of Little Ease housed in the old Town Hall; Walter Bagehot who worked alongside the American President Woodrow Wilson; Peony Valley and willow-growing and of course the making of cider.

So, here we are at our mid-way point of the Trail. Twenty-five miles walked and another twenty-five still to trek. What have we discovered today? What will we discover tomorrow?

Until reaching Kingsbury Episcopi the countryside and its flora has been much the same as we've seen since our start at Chedington. Hamstone buildings have been very much in evidence and then, all of a sudden, the colour of the stone changed to the grey-blue of Blue Lias. Additional industries to those we'd already discovered were the river trade and the brewing of cider, and there are more to come as we travel. The landscape changed dramatically too as we moved toward Thorney and Langport. It changed to moorland as underneath our feet lay Blue Lias topped with clay and then peat, the latter good for water retention, which over the centuries has created the perfect habitat for reeds, rushes and sedges. And this is where I've asked myself, what is it that's caused this to happen?

You now know the answer to that: our geology!

*Pack horse teams were usually a group of about forty horses all carrying goods by panniers: three hundred and sixty-five pounds, the weight of a wool sack. As a journey example, let's use London to Carlisle. En route the horses using horrendously poor roads would have taken around three weeks, today's juggernauts would take one day!

Langport to Bridgwater

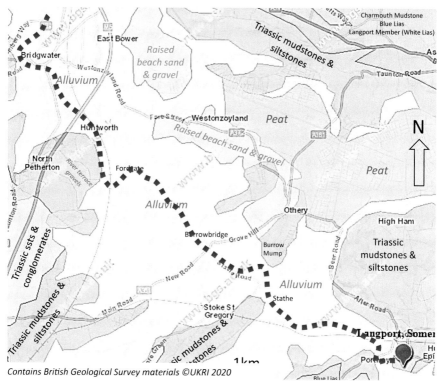

Contains British Geological Survey materials ©UKRI 2020

Langport Viaduct

Chapter 5
Langport to Bridgwater 19.5k (12.2mls)

On the last part of the previous leg of our journey we stood on Great Bow Bridge at Langport looking in the direction of the railway viaduct which now we're now standing by. From here we're able to see the Lock Keeper's cottage built of the stone we now know as Blue Lias. The cottage on the river bank is parallel to the river and the long-abandoned and derelict site of a one-time lock, one of three on the Parrett. The first is at Thorney Mill, the second here at Langport and the third at Oath. Later we'll be walking close to the confluence of the Rivers Parrett and Tone. The River Tone had several locks too, the nearest to the Parrett as far as I'm aware is close to Stanmoor a mile or so upstream from the Tone's confluence. Approximately three miles beyond is Newbridge, considered to be the final point of tidal effects from the sea. The last evidence of these same effects on the Parrett is at Oath.

During the early 1830s the Parrett Navigation Company was formed to oversee the building of the locks, plus the rebuilding of Great Bow Bridge. This enabled those who earned their living on the rivers to be able to ply their trade without having to rely on the turn of the tide.

Apparently one of the lock keepers was rather partial to his 'scrumpy', as cider is known locally, and due to the many pubs and other ale houses in Langport, was able to enjoy his pint or two with happy abandonment, in which case he would often have been the worse for wear. Sadly, his family discovered him one morning lying face down in the river, drowned.

A little about the viaduct. This is all part of the Great Western Railway or as some fondly call it, God's Wonderful Railway. Certainly, Isambard Kingdom Brunel would have felt this way, for this was his invention. Built during 1906, the line carried express trains from London to Taunton and the West, bypassing Bath and Bristol. The foundations for the bridge and viaduct had to be sunk to a depth of more than forty-five feet (this varies with each reference book), through peat and clay to reach stable ground. When the line was tested for its ability to carry trains, disaster struck. The first section of the arched viaduct collapsed, whereupon a special and strengthening girder was installed.

During 2020, millions of pounds were spent reinforcing this section of the line. No doubt it will be necessary again in the future because of the ground's instability.

Back-tracking a little, close to Muchelney and Westover we discovered the remains of the branch railway bridge and learned that the line started by joining the main line at Langport. Now you can see where. Here as you stand by the viaduct and look across the river to the sewage works, the connection of both lines was a little beyond that.

The depth that the railway stanchions needed to be sunk, gives us an insight into what lies under our feet; a topping of unstable peat lies on the rather more stable alluvial clay and Blue Lias. In some places the peat can be as much as ninety feet thick but this is generally found to the north of the Poldens. Here there is peat, which is still dug, but not to the same extent as in the past. Today peat is no longer used for fuel but used as compost and in the making of grow bags.

Have you ever wondered why this area is known as Sedgemoor? I've always associated the non-acidic peat where sedges grow well, as being the reason for the name *Sedge* moor. However, as we discovered at Merriott, it has come from an Old Norse personal name, '*marsh of a man called Sicga*' with an Old English suffix of mor which today is moor. In wetlands such as we're now in, you may find this area called by some as a 'mere' a word of O.E. origin. It is interesting that within records dated 1165 it was documented as *Segamere*.

As we stand here in what I'd describe as a rather large, flat-bottomed bowl, in places only six to ten feet above sea level, look at the surrounding topography. Whichever way you turn are ridges of hills, from which rivers and their tributaries flow to eventually feed the waters of the Parrett and the lands around it. Ask yourself with all we've discovered about these hills so far, what is the bedrock of these areas? Limestone. Yes, the waters do contain lime but in the form of calcium hydroxide in solution, which helps to neutralise the acid in the peat. Later, we'll learn a little about willow-growing and why it grows so well here on Sedgemoor. Peat moss which is acidic, is a welcome home for both heathers and cannabis!

The height of the surrounding hills above sea level, with approximate distances, are:

The Brendon Hills to the north-north-west, reaching a height of 1388 feet, 30 miles; the Quantocks to the north-west, reaching a height of 1261 feet, 20 miles; the Poldens to the north, reaching a height of 260 feet, 5 miles; the Mendips to the north-north-east, reaching a height of 1068 feet, 20–25 miles; and last but not least are the Dorset Hills to the south, where we started this trek at 600 feet.

This distance, as we know, is 25 miles.

We'll discover a little more about these hills and their rivers as we approach Burrow Mump close to the confluence of the Rivers Parrett and Tone.

And now to Monks Leaze Clyse, yet another name to ponder on. The monks from Athelney, Muchelney or Glastonbury would have worked these lands, hence the first part of the overall name. Clyse bothered me for some time but I discovered that it is a local term for a type of sluice. This is a one-way valve that allows fresh water to drain out into the tidal river, when the level of the river is below the drain. As the latter is a one-way system and even when the river level is above the drain, sea water is unable to enter. After passing Bridgwater we'll be able to see several more clyses but these are less obvious than this one.

Since the 1970s Monks Leaze Clyse has been connected to the Parrett by a flood relief channel known as the River Sowy, meaning sea-way. Eventually this connects to King's Sedgemoor Drain. The latter was constructed at the turn of the 18th century to help drain much of Sedgemoor by taking its waters to meet and flow into the Parrett at Dunball, just north of Bridgwater. These waters then flow out toward the sea.

In addition to the River Sowy, spillways were built. These are specifically-formed river banks which have been reduced in height by approximately 12 inches with the back slope leaning gently toward the land. These measures help to prevent erosion as the water overflows from the river. Moving on toward Oath Lock, you'll be walking along one of these spillways.

As we approached Langport we were talking about White Lias and Bowden's Quarry (now Lovell's) which is above us and to our right. It's time to note that the area there is wooded and becomes even more so as we look toward Aller. Why has this happened when here where we're standing has very few trees? As with the sedge liking the peat, the trees love the limestone. I find it is so exciting to begin to discover that all around us is the result of what's under our feet: the bedrock, the geology.

Whilst we walk toward Burrow Mump we'll pass Oath (Old English for river bank) and the lock here, which marks the tidal limit on the River Parrett, although before its installation the river, so I've been told was tidal to Langport and beyond. The electronically counter-balanced lifting gates were installed during 1938 and form a weir across the river. At either side are flaps (clyses), which close when the tide raises the water level downstream. During heavy rainfall the gates are raised to allow the water to pass downstream and away as quickly as possible, but during a dry summer the gates are lowered. This is to keep river levels upstream sufficiently high to meet the needs of agriculture, recreation and nature conservation.

En route you may catch a glimpse of the Wellington Monument constructed in honour of the Duke of Wellington after his successful battle at Waterloo during June 1815. Approximately twenty-five miles west-south-west and standing on the Blackdown Hills (1033ft at the highest point), the site of the monument will offer superb views if you decide to visit.

Approaching Stathe – and having said previously that we are walking in a mainly treeless area – hey presto here is a man-made circle of willows and firs. This is most probably a Victorian hide acting as a duck decoy. Quite often, cormorants and Berwick swans can be seen here too.

Stathe Bridge is a good place to stop for a while as there is a lot to tell and a lot to see.

Stathe is Old English for landing place and here at the bridge is an alternative route to reach Burrow Mump. This is approximately ten miles, rather more than the route we're going to take which is a mere two miles. The longer route, although much by road, is full of interest. There are willow-boiling chimneys to be seen, the monument at Athelney to Alfred the Great (site of his abbey), plus there are spectacular views over the flood plain of the River Tone from Windmill Hill. Nearby is the Willow and Wetland Centre which has its own museum showing how today's landscape has been created from marsh and swamp, together with illustrations of wetland flowers, insects and birds. There are sections on traditional industries based on local plants such as teasles', which I'll return to in a moment after a little about willows.

Willows bring us back to what lies beneath our feet: clay and peat. Together these retain moisture which is essential to the willows' growth. A newly-planted bed will take two to three years to establish and, with good husbandry will last for approximately twenty-five years. During November the withies are harvested, and depending on how they are treated, different colours can be obtained – white, buff and brown – white for the cricket bat, buff for baskets and brown for hurdles and those used for spiling, which is a way of stabilising river banks. The inner frames of the Military bearskin hats are formed from willow and, the story is told, that willow potties were used by ladies at times of personal crisis when attending church services! I must admit to questioning this!

In 1970, during peat excavations, an important discovery by Ray Sweet was of a prehistoric wooden trackway (named the Sweet Track), constructed by Neolithic farmers during 3807BC. Willow was found in the mile-long section that travels from Shapwick Heath toward Westhay and Meare. Willow has other uses too. It creates a good charcoal for artists and is an important ingredient of gunpowder.

Now it's the turn of the teasel. We first mentioned these when we were near the Hamstone culvert close to Haselbury Mill. Those we saw were the common teasel. A remedy of the past to cure sore eyes was to bathe them using water caught in the cup-shaped leaves. The heads were and still are used to raise the nap on cloth, but the best for this is the Fullers Teasel. Fulling is a means of removing grease from cloth which we discussed during the first day of our trek. The Fullers Teasel has a smaller head than the common teasel. Its head is harder with long, spiny hooked bracts, and once the cloth is clean and dry, these are used for raising the nap on cloth such as billiard tables, velvet and top hats. In the past these plants were grown locally for use on the Levels, but today many are imported from Poland.

From the bridge here at Stathe you'll be able to see one of a few remaining brick willow-boiling chimneys on the opposite side of the river and, although we can't see it, a little further

Willow Boiling Chimney, Stathe

back and alongside the road is one of the many brick pumping stations; this one built during 1944.

Looking in the opposite direction we can see the tower of Aller church with woodlands behind it approximately a mile away. It is a fascinating church which contains some beautiful Norman work. The construction of the bell tower is worth seeing too. However, the church and its surrounding area is mainly remembered for its association with Alfred the Great: – the place where he christened Guthrum, King of the Danes, plus several of Guthrum's oels (senior officers') during 878 AD. With the Danes finally defeated by Alfred at the battle of Edington, came the much sought-after peace treaty at Wedmore. Alfred was then King of all England.

I mentioned the Battle of Langport briefly whilst we were in the town, but Aller wasn't spared involvement. Oliver Cromwell and General Massey stayed a night here during July 1645 along with foot soldiers who were billeted around the village. This brings me to the next leg of our journey as we walk alongside the river around an area which is known as War Moor. Does this mean that a skirmish occurred here by the riverside during the battle?

Walking onward and toward Burrow Mump this would have been an area where barges re-started their journeys upstream from Burrowbridge by utilising the incoming and fast-flowing tidal waters, plus using the power of rope-tethered horses led by a young boy. Later and as we approach Bridgwater, we'll be walking more towpaths and it's here we'll come to realise just how much impact the rope-tethered horse made to our busy riversides and canals.

We've already met the adjoining River Yeo which loses its identity to the Parrett at Langport. Now we're meeting the River Tone which also loses its identity to the Parrett. We mentioned earlier the rivers flowing from the surrounding hills and here we see the part they played and still play in creating this ever-growing river and the landscape we see around us here today.

The significant limey-rich rivers flowing down to the Somerset Levels are the Tone which is twenty-one miles in length and starts its life at Beverton Pond near Huish Champflower. I just have to search for the meaning of this beautiful name. Huish is Old English for a measure of land sufficient to feed a family: Champflower is a manorial affix from the 13th century Champflur family.

The River Brue, its source close to Alfred's Tower and Stourhead, flows for

31 miles to reach the sea a little to the north of Stert Point and the mouth of the Parrett.

As to the Mendips, Poldens and Blackdowns there are no major rivers, but smaller rivers would no doubt flow to feed and swell the waters of the two large waterways we're able to see here today. In a short while when you're standing at the top of the Mump, you'll be able to gain a much better view of this area.

In front of us is a single-span bridge built in 1826. This was at that time, the only crossing of the Parrett between Langport and Bridgwater before the building of the M5 motorway. The road (Taunton to Glastonbury) ahead of us was turnpiked until 1945. Little is left of the Toll House for us to see. In times before the bridge this part of the river was at low tide, a fording point for carts, thanks to the firm bedrock of Mercia Mudstone, formerly known as Keuper Marl.

This is one of the oldest rock formations that we've come across since we began our trek forming during the Triassic Period (250 to 200 million years ago). A pre-dominantly red rock it is used in the building industry as it contains gypsum which is used to create plaster. It is also good as a fertiliser. Rock salt is present too, but at great depth. Toward the end of our overall journey, we'll be in the vicinity of Puriton ammunition factory, where, in 1910, a borehole was drilled to obtain the salt there. This was then pumped to the surface and used as brine for domestic and industrial purposes. Today and further afield in Cheshire, Triassic salt is still mined and put to use as a de-icing agent for roads.

A natural stopping place for both carts and barges, suggests the reason for the development of Burrowbridge and its pub, the King Alfred, thought to date from the 1600s at a time when the river trade was booming. Think of yourselves today taking a long journey with young children who are constantly saying, "I'm thirsty, I'm hungry" and more. You'd find as good a place to stop as the King Alfred pub would have been to the boatmen and carriers. With the pub in mind, we could ourselves share a welcome pint. We'll certainly need one after our 75 ft high climb to the top of Burrow Mump!

Why does Burrow Mump stand high over the surrounding and flat landscape of the Levels? It is due to the bedrock geology. The nearby riverbed's alluvium is underlain by Mercia Mudstone. The Mump's lower levels are of Triassic sandstone capped by this very same mudstone. Over millions of years the overlying layers of the succeeding Jurassic and Cretaceous periods, have been worn away by the ravages of time and weather.

Let's now turn to the Merry Monks of the 12th and 13th centuries. Or were they merry when they toiled long and hard building flood defence walls around the Mump? Why did they build them?

At that time local wool was recognised worldwide for its extremely high quality. Exporting wool was a major boost to the country's economy and one of great importance to the monks. By creating flood defence walls to curb the waters of the Rivers Tone and Parrett, more pasture land was made available to feed more sheep and these in turn produced more wool, which made more money!

When we were at the start of the second leg of our journey, we were walking through lush pasturelands which fed flocks of sheep. At the time I mentioned that we'd discover later how the monks spent their extra income. Here is the answer. Extra money enabled the monks to build the magnificent Somerset churches, most of them complete with lofty towers. We've seen St Bartholomew's at Crewkerne and mentioned All Saints at Martock. There are numerous churches in the villages around, churches we've not seen, but the majority built on the profits of the wool trade. It is of no surprise then that the monks took on the onerous task of building the flood walls. As we've walked from Stathe Bridge to Burrowbridge we've been walking along the remains of one of those walls, Southlake Wall. Other walls in the vicinity are Baltmoor, Chalice and Tapping.

The original chapel of St Michael at the top of the Mump dates from the 15th century if not earlier. The ruinous state of it today possibly dates to the Civil War when Royalist troops made a vain stand on the hill after the Battle of Langport in 1645.

Do read the inscription plaque on the south wall of the building. The words *Sumorsaete ealle,* now used as the Somerset County Council motto, are taken from a passage in the Anglo-Saxon Chronicle for the year 878 AD:

'King Alfred with a small force … made a stronghold at Athelney, and he and the section of the people of Somerset which was nearest to it proceeded to fight from the stronghold against the enemy. Then in the seventh week after Easter he rode east of Selwood, and there came to meet him 'All the People of Somerset and of Wiltshire and Hampshire.'

And last but not least we cannot forget the views: the Quantock Hills in the distance, with a little closer Athelney Monument marking the site of the abbey founded by Alfred the Great to the west. St Mary's Hamstone church spire at Bridgwater lies to the north and, to the northeast, Glastonbury Tor. Look out too for Burton Pynsent monument to the south.

Time to move on now alongside the river toward the pumping station at Westonzoyland. This is an area where large red-brick houses are dotted along the riverside. Who owned them I ask myself? Were they again connected with affluent merchants of the river trade? Look out for Manor Farm with its beautiful Italianate window. Notice too, the blocked windows here. I'm assuming these were the result of the window tax of 1696 to which houses with over seven windows were subject. This tax was repealed during 1851 and it was then that the production of Bristol Blue glass increased as this was not taxable.

Hale's Farm and the house behind it are both of interest, the rear one in particular. When we were viewing the workers' cottages at the Parrett Works, we looked particularly at the roof tiles, and I commented that Bridgwater's brick and tile industry was beginning to make its mark. Now we're even closer. The main house is constructed with redbrick. The roof has been covered by Bridgwater triple delta tiles. The building behind the farm has to the ends of the ridge tiles, finials, a decorative tile which stands upright and forms the terminal at the top of the gable end of the house. Very often they represent leaves or lilies, but can also be moulded as animals. Think back to the lock-up at Kingsbury Episcopi where we saw a ball finial.

On the opposite side of the river is Moorland House another large redbrick building complete with attractive sash windows. The height of fashion during the Georgian era, these were the 'must have' windows for those who could afford them. Both the origin and dates of sash windows are unknown.

Tansy is a plant we've not seen before. A member of the daisy family, it grows readily in this area. The leaves are bitter and pungent but used in the past for curing phlegm and worms. Mixed with egg, milk and flour and cooked as an omelette this possibly made the potion more palatable. A word of caution as with other medicinal plants too. *Always check with a qualified herbalist before using them.*

For those of you who wish to discover a little more about Westonzoyland, a short diversion needs to be made. Maybe the first step might be to the Sedgemoor Inn? Here, it is said, there's the ghost of a Royalist soldier whose plodding feet can be heard in one of the bedrooms. Other visits could be to the church and the pumping station.

We've already seen or mentioned five pumping stations, the latest at Northmoor built during 1868. You'll now see on the opposite side of the river and ahead of us, Westonzoyland pumping station's tall chimney. This was the first station to be built on the moor (1827). Nowadays it's a museum complete with a fully working beam engine. The names of companies such as James Easton and Easton and Amos crop up here and will be familiar to those of you who are lovers of the 'Steam Age.'

Westonzoyland is remembered chiefly for the events of 1685 when the rebel Protestant army, followers of the Duke of Monmouth (illegitimate son of Charles II) were defeated at the Battle of Sedgemoor by the royal army of Roman Catholic James II. The battle, the last to be fought on English soil, claimed approximately five hundred rebel prisoners. The wounded and dying were herded into the nearby church and without doubt covered the floors with blood and gore. Several prisoners were hanged (some reputedly naked) outside of the church without a trial. Rebels killed on the battlefield were interred within a mass grave. For those who were tried by the notorious Bloody Judge Jefferies, their sentences were severe. Around seven hundred were transported to the West Indies to endure ten years of hard labour, and another three hundred and more were condemned to death.

St Mary's Church here at Westonzoyland is one of beauty. A Grade I listed building constructed of Blue Lias, it has a magnificent tower complete with sculptures called Hunky Punks. These are considered to be clad with woolly coats, thought to represent the lucrative wool trade. The interior of the church has a beautifully-carved timber roof, one of many throughout our Somerset churches. These by their own merits are worth viewing – craftsmanship at its best.

Some of you may be wondering why the name Westonzoyland? As with 'ney', 'zoy' also indicates island. Grouped together these three villages, Othery, Middlezoy and Westonzoyland became known in the past as Sowy Island. Sowy meaning a seaway. These villages sit on a ridge of slightly higher ground where gravel is evident. It is fertile land and as free from flooding would most probably have been cultivated by the Saxons. During the 13th century more than seven hundred acres of meadow land were reclaimed making it sufficiently stable for buildings.

As we continue our journey alongside the Parrett, if the tide is low look at the amount of sludge on the river bed. We'll talk about this a little later as it is important, yes important! House martins use sludge to create their nests which have the most decorative edges to their openings. Looked at closely they appear like a miniature woven rope. The nests can be seen on the eaves of nearby houses.

St. Mary's Church, Westonzoyland

After passing the Thatcher's Arms, you'll be walking alongside a tiny tributary of the Parrett. Growing here are beautiful reeds which when in flower during late summer have delicate heads of purple to brown, shown off at their best in a gentle breeze. These Phragmites Reeds can be harvested and used for thatching. For those of you who have a love of birds, the larger reed beds are home to the bearded tit, reed warbler, marsh harrier and sometimes the elusive bittern.

A quiet lane takes us toward a bridge over the Great Western Railway line (Bridgwater to Taunton) and beyond it, the Bridgwater and Taunton canal. The lane will take you past a house constructed in what appears to be red sandstone. This is the home of Barney Rubble and the Flintstone family. I'm not joking, this is fact!

So far on this journey we've been walking along field footpaths, bridle ways and quiet lanes. Now we're about to walk along the towpath of the Bridgwater and Taunton canal which opened during 1827 to commercial craft carrying goods such as coal, iron and agricultural goods. But, as happened at Langport with the opening of the branch railway line causing the demise of the river trade there, the railways here caused the closure of this canal during 1907.

If you feel inspired you can walk the complete route of approximately 24 km (15 miles) from Bridgwater Docks to Firepool in Taunton. Not only is it interesting but it is scenic too. You might be lucky enough to see a kingfisher.

Here at Fordgate we've reached one of the swing bridges which were removed during the 2nd World War, their iron being used to help the war efforts. Since then they have been replaced with wood. Here too is another house built of apparent red sandstone, although weathering has changed it to a rusty brown. It is possibly Ilfracombe Slate, coming from the quarry at Treborough in the Brendon Hills. The overall formation comprises of slates and limestone of marine origin along with sandstone and slates with a shallow marine or deltaic origin. Look at the construction of the stone, it is so very different in appearance from the Hamstone and Blue Lias we've become accustomed to.

It might be of interest to you to briefly mention a little about geology's three main rock formations. Slates such as used in the house we've just seen, are metamorphic rocks which means that overtime they've been changed by heat or pressure. Igneous rock, such as Granite was formed by hot and liquid magma which then cooled to create a close grained, hard rock. Take a trip to Wells Cathedral to see numerous types of stone used in the building, but inside, look for the granite pillars. Sedimentary rock which has bands of different rocks laid down one upon another, we've seen as Hamstone at Ham Hill. This was used in the construction of Montacute House only a short distance away. Blue Lias is also a sedimentary rock and as we saw, was used to construct the body of the church at Kingsbury Episcopi.

Let's now see what flora has grown as a result of the rock and soil formations here at Fordgate. Bullrushes (reed-mace) grow in waterlogged areas. Their stems are straight and jointless which makes them ideal for plaiting and weaving into baskets, mats and chair seats.

Water lilies, I've known as brandy balls, deriving their name from their smell which is similar to wine.

Deadly nightshade, or *Belladonna* has been used as a hallucinatory drug. Used externally to relieve neuralgia and in very small doses as an antidote to opium. Belladonna means 'beautiful lady', the name thought to have come from Italy as ladies there used the water distilled from the plant to dilate their pupils and make their eyes more brilliant.

Dog Rose, also known as *Rosa Canina*. The latter part of the word comes from the Latin word 'canis' meaning dog, as it was thought by the Romans that the root could be used as an antidote to cure rabies. The hips are rich in vitamin C and can also be used to make a refreshing but slightly sour tea or to make a piquant marmalade.

Fennel is another member of the Umbelliferae family, smells similar to aniseed and can be used to flavour fish and egg dishes. Roman gladiators used to mix fennel with food as a stimulant. The seeds are sometimes used to make liquors which supposedly promote digestion.

Horseradish grows here as it does around Langport, ready to be used for roast beef and Yorkshire pudding.

Travellers' joy or old man's beard (Clematis family) needs to be handled with care as its juices can cause skin irritations. During Victorian times, so the story is told, beggars would rub their skin with these juices to entice money from the pockets of the soft-hearted.

And now, a few birds. We'll more than likely see swans. There is only one of the eight breeds of swan which stays in Britain all year round. This is the mute swan with an overall bright orange beak – mute because they are quieter than other swans and use display as their language. Moorhens and coots are here too and most probably we'll see herons and cormorants looking for fish, which here tend to be roach and tench and offer fishermen hours of enjoyment. Enjoyment is available as well for those who love boating, as since the 1994 restoration, the canal has been open end-to-end for all to enjoy.

En route there are the remains of several pillboxes, all part of the Taunton Stop Line which ran from north of the mouth of the River Parrett at Highbridge to Axmouth in Devon, a distance of 80 km (50 miles). This was a defensive line built during the 2nd World War to stop the enemy entering the country from the west using large armoured fighting vehicles. A vast array of defences were created, not only along canals such as this, but railway

Pillbox, Fordgate

embankments too. Pillboxes were installed with light machine guns and some with anti-blast walls. Elsewhere there were anti-tank gun emplacements such as concrete posts and cubes. Donyatt, a village close to the town of Ilminster, is a good place to see these. Close by and situated on Donyatt Halt platform is the most beautiful bronze sculpture of Dorothy, a war- time evacuee. This figure is very moving.

Back to the canal where we've come to the end of today's journey.

Our start for Section Six will be here too, when we'll be joining a canal link opened in 1841 to enable craft to access Bridgwater Docks.

However, if we retrace our steps for a very short way, we could enjoy an end of the day drink at the Boat and Anchor pub. How about mulling over what we've all shared and experienced during the day?

At Langport at the start our day, we were in an area of Blue Lias, alluvial clay and peat, discovering the power of the neutralising limy waters flowing from the surrounding hills down into the basin-like Somerset Levels, creating soil conditions suitable for the willow industry. At Burrowbridge we learned about the firmness and stability of the Mercia Mudstone which underlies the riverbed, an aid to carts transporting goods to ford the River Parrett at low tide, the only way to cross before the bridge was constructed. Standing at the top of Burrow Mump beneath our feet was again Mercia Mudstone.

Man's attempts to prevent flooding, or at least to drain flood waters away, became obvious too, seeing flood banks built by the monks plus the later pumping stations of the 19th and 20th centuries. Houses constructed of brick became more evident as we walked toward Bridgwater. At Weston-zoyland we learned of the bloody Battle of Sedgemoor. We've also shared an interesting and scenic walk alongside part of the canal, seeing birds, flowers, bridges plus evidence of 2nd World War defences. There is more to be seen on the next and last leg of our journey, but that's to discover then, not today.

Enjoy your pint!

Bridgwater to Stert Point

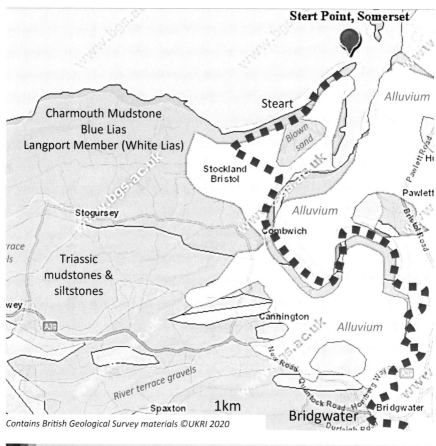

Stert Point, Somerset

Alluvium

Steart

Charmouth Mudstone
Blue Lias
Langport Member (White Lias)

Blown sand

Stockland Bristol

Pawlett Hi

Pawlett

Stogursey

Alluvium

Combwich

Triassic mudstones & siltstones

rrace ls

wey

A39

Cannington

Alluvium

New Road

Quantock Road

Homberg Way

A3?

River terrace gravels

Spaxton   1km

Bridgwater

Durleigh Rd

Contains British Geological Survey materials ©UKRI 2020

Bridgwater roof tiles, finials and barge boards

Chapter 6
Bridgwater to Stert Point 19.5k (12.2mls)

Here at Hamp bridge is the start of the urban part of our walk. We're parallel with the river at which point the canal now veers off slightly to the left of us, a loop created during 1841 leading to the then newly formed docks. There are old clay pits to our left and factory buildings to our right. But there is beauty here, typical red brick canal bridges. A few have their numbered plates on them but sad to say many have been stolen or vandalised.

So far on our journey the only town we've visited has been Langport, a small country market town. Now we meet the industrial town of Bridgwater. Whilst walking beside the Bridgwater and Taunton canal we've walked beneath the M5 flyover to reach Crossway's Swing-bridge. What I find of interest here is the platform of superbly-laid bricks, using both engineering and house bricks. Take note of how they are shaped. If you're interested in seeing other uses of these, a detour to visit Victoria Road is well worthwhile. There you will see rows of terraced houses. Coping bricks top the garden walls and finials stand on the gables of each house. Decorated door surrounds have been created by using small and curved bricks, whereas today the corners would be squared. Window lintels have moulded flower patterns emphasised by coloured paint. Just under the eaves is a decorative way of using either brick or the ends of roof timbers. These houses with their uniform front bay windows were beautifully built to accommodate the numerous employees of the lucrative brick and tile industry.

Hamp canal bridge is the first of several we'll see along this route. To me their arched shapes over the water, combined with mellow red Bridgwater bricks, create a feeling of peace and tranquillity. Today, for those of us who take canal holidays 'simply messing about on boats', wandering the waterways at a leisurely pace is in itself a peaceful occupation. But, think back one hundred years and more to those who used the canals to earn a living by carrying a variety of goods to earn a crust, very often tired, wet, cold and most probably hungry too.

Now is a good time to mention the alluvial soils we've been walking through since leaving Langport. These consist of clay, silt and gravels carried up-stream by fast-flowing tidal waters, and then deposited on the riverbed as the flow of the water slows. Here and for a couple of miles ahead, this area is particularly rich in fine particles of alumina and silica. These materials were extremely useful in the past as they were used to create the Bath Brick, which was sold and used as a scouring block, before the advent of the scouring pads. The importance of the slime was twofold. By collecting the slime for bricks, the river bed was also dredged, necessary to keep the channel clear for shipping in the days when Bridgwater was a busy port. The slime was a free material which meant that only labour costs were incurred – a win, win situation!

Returning to the canal, we'll be able to see to our right the 175 ft Ham-stone spire of St Mary's Church. From here, so the tale is told, the Duke of Monmouth climbed the tower to overlook the battlefield at Westonzoy-land, where on the following day he and his rebels were defeated by the Royalist army.

We'll also see the remains of clay pits, industrial buildings all in the vicin-ity of the site of a Franciscan Friary in use by friars' during the mid-13th century. In the meadows surrounding Durleigh Brook, excavations during 2003 exposed the remains of the friars' church. However, as with so many religious establishments during the 16th century the monastery was dis-solved by Henry VIII.

Of interest to those of you wanting to discover more about the Dissolution of the Monasteries, when we were at Ham Hill, I mentioned that this was the end of the twenty-eight-mile Leland Trail. This follows part of the route Leland took after being commissioned by Henry VIII to seek out wealthy monasteries and abbeys. The journey took Leland throughout the country and the knowledge he gained en route enabled Henry to forge ahead de-stroying these religious buildings and plundering their assets.

The next outstanding canal section for me is Albert's Cutting, constructed as part of the canal's new loop during 1841. The walls to either side of the canal are constructed of Red Sandstone. Since 1951 these walls have been given extra support by enormous wooden beams, but today these are in need of repair. In the early days of the Parrett Trail these beams were carved with the following poem, the carving now needing attention too.

Albert's Cutting

Navigators

Hard Graft Sinew and Bone
Jolt of the Pick Crack of the Hammer
Iron and Stone Red Quantock
We came and went
Our Legacy
A Boat Coming Clean Through the Hill

These words go a little way toward helping us understand the hard labour the 'navvies' undertook. Their skills without the aid of diggers, pneumatic drills or lorries to take away unwanted soil, are as stated by the words of the poem, their legacy here and, at the Docks ahead. But let us remember the railways we have today, these are their legacy too.

At Burrowbridge we were talking about the towpath by the river and the impact of the rope-tethered horses on our canals. Now all will be revealed. Here at Albert's Cutting, look at the cast-iron shields at the lower section of the bridge arches. Why were they made and what were they used for?

Look closely at these shields and you'll see several indentations in the metal, indentations created to guide the ropes of tethered horses plodding the towpath whilst pulling barges laden with goods. The shields would have reduced friction too, saving wear and tear on the ropes. Now take a look at the bridge. Look at the brickwork done by skilled craftsmen. This is what is known as a 'skew' bridge, which is one that is built at an oblique angle rather than the usual right angle. This must have been a laborious task when cutting the bricks to size and shape as there was no modern technology and, as before at Albert's Cutting, no modern-day equipment for the navvies to use to build the bridge. Today these bridges, again the legacy of the 'navvies', have become structures of beauty for us all to enjoy.

Newtown Lock, Bridgwater

For a while now I've mentioned Bridgwater's brick and tile industry. As we near Newtown Lock at the southern entry to the Dock, look ahead where you'll see in the distance the one remaining brick kiln used by Barham Bros Yard, until the early part of the 20th century. Now look to your left and you'll see Bowring's Mill. The brickwork is a mixture of red and white on both the main building and the tall, magnificent octagonal chimney. Was this an advertisement for the brick industry I wonder?

With the decline of the brick and tile industry during the early 20th century, over the years dereliction of the yard set in. By the 1990s, Sedgemoor Council and Somerset County Council rescued the remaining Grade II listed

Brick kiln in the distance, near the docks

kiln. Alongside they created a building based on a former tile-drying shed which was then opened as the Brick and Tile Museum. If you visit, you'll be able to see, apart from a variety of bricks, tiles and finials, the inner parts of a kiln, which when full took forty-four thousand bricks. Cooling time for these after they'd been fired was a fortnight, which explains the need for several kilns in one yard.

Around the Docks are former warehouses, one now utilised as a pub – maybe a chance for a pint whilst overlooking the marina. The initial aim here, sadly not achieved, was to create moorings for one-hundred and twenty craft which would have brought both employment and welcome income to Bridgwater.

At the confluence of the Rivers Parrett and Yeo we discussed the scene as it must have been one-hundred years ago, with numerous barges carrying goods to Ilchester and Gawbridge. At Hamp bridge we spoke again of the lives of the bargees who a century ago worked on this canal.

For a third time here at Bridgwater Docks opened during 1841, let's think about this area during the mid-19th century as it must have looked with men loading and unloading ships coming in from the Bristol Channel. Using the newly-opened dock that was designed as a 'floating harbour' made life so much easier than before when they were completely reliant on the tidal river plus when the tide was high. Men were now able to continue their work at any time of the day.

The Parrett was navigable for boats of up to 400 tons, although the wide tidal range meant that for much of the time no ship of more than 100 tons could approach the docks until the next spring tide plus the Parrett Bore. Apart from having to wait in the estuary for these tides, another difficulty was the need to employ 'hobblers' who manually pulled the ships into port, often covering a distance of two miles. Imagine the celebrations that must have occurred when the new dock with its 'floating harbour' was completed.

The Parrett Bore coincides with the spring tides during March or April and September and usually occurs at the times of the spring and autumn equinoxes. This immense surge of water raises the usual high tides by approximately 6 – 15 ft. As we discovered before, the power of these waters can be seen inland as far as Oath Lock.

The Bristol Channel tides are the second highest in the world, approximately 47 ft above normal levels. The highest occur in Nova Scotia with an extra 68 ft. Approaching this is the massive Severn Bore at 50 ft above its normal levels.

During the 15th century goods being exported were wool and agricultural produce. During the 17th century exported wheat became a good source of income. By the mid-19th century, approximately eight million bricks were exported to America, the Middle East and China. Coming into the port, there was coal from Wales and timber from North America, plus dairy products.

Around the dock are the remains of lifting gear and to the northern end another lock plus a 'bascule bridge'. For those of you who love 'steam powered' vehicles there are the remains of an old railway line for you to discover, part of the Somerset and Dorset line or unkindly called the Slow and Dirty.

There is so much to explore in and around Bridgwater. Tourist Information Town Trail leaflets give you a flavour of the town's industrial past including the Blake Museum thought to be the birthplace of Admiral Blake much admired by Nelson, the Brick and Tile Museum, Castle St 18th century and Grade 1 listed, St Mary's church and so much more and:- if you visit during early November, you could be a part of the huge crowds who gather to watch the famous Bridgwater Carnival.

Alongside a huge curve in the river with its bed of mud and sand, is Dunball Wharf. This was created by Bridgwater coal merchants during 1844. Today this is the only part of the Port of Bridgwater still in commercial use. Again, built by the coal merchants during 1876, was the railway link to the Bristol and Exeter Railway, originally operated as a horse-drawn tramway. Today the wharf is used for landing stone products, marine sand and gravels dredged from the Bristol Channel. However, tourism plays its part here too. Dunball is a boarding place for day trippers to Lundy Island aboard the Balmoral steamship. Travelling this way gives an insight into the narrow navigational channels that are available to ships, whilst sailing the tidal River Parrett.

Just beyond Langport we met Monks Leaze Clyse. Here and along this part of the route, we'll meet Stallington's Clyse and the start of a footpath which takes you to Cannington. The Agricultural College here is one of great repute. Both Cannington houses and religious buildings are constructed using Red Sandstone.

The Benedictine Nunnery built during the 12th century was dissolved during 1538. Whilst occupied by the nuns another story has evolved. Is it true? The village has a pub named the Flying Spirit which it's said has an underground tunnel leading to the Nunnery, through which the 'naughty nuns' escaped to sample the brews in what was then most probably an ale house. Happy times!

Looking across the river from Combwich you'll be able to see Pawlett and its church: – within which are box pews. If you were to stand on Knowle Hill not far from Bridgwater, you'd be visiting the spot where James II viewed the site of his victorious battle at Westonzoyland. Looking back, St Mary's church spire stands way above the majority of Bridgwater's buildings. Inland can be seen Cannington Hill Fort another high point of the Levels – 260 ft above sea level. The fort was occupied by Bronze and Iron Age people and later by the Romans followed by the Saxons. The cemetery here is thought to be late Roman, early Saxon and contained several hundred bodies.

Let's think back to the very first leg of our journey. At its end we reached Merriott locally known as Mert. Combwich is pronounced as 'Cummidge'.

Cumb is Old English for short, broad, open valley. *Wich* is possibly 'homestead' of Romano-British times.

For those of you who love flora and fauna this area is particularly good for coastal plants: succulents, lichens, starry saxifrage, purple loosestrife and mignonette. In the 'mud sculptures' (my name for the mud's formations) of the riverbed when the tide is low there are oyster catchers, avocets, shellducks and white egrets. If like me your knowledge of plants and birds is limited, this is definitely an area to visit with a botanist and ornithologist. A visit to the Nature Reserve at Steart a little farther on would be invaluable.

Approaching Combwich our first sight is of the massive jetty. The original one was built during the 1960s to accommodate heavy goods being brought by sea for use on the construction of the first nuclear power station at Hinkley Point. Now, during 2020, with the development of Hinkley C, the jetty is being enlarged to take even heavier loads. It is enormous!

Back to the soils again. Here White Lias skirts the western side of the river and to the east is Alluvium, both extremely fertile areas. During Roman times Combwich became an important port and continued to be so until Bridgwater took prominence during the 16th century when the exporting of cloth was at its height. Since the early first century and until fairly recent times the lands here consisted of meadows, pasture and arable fields. Livestock included cattle, pigs, sheep and poultry. By the 16th century there was not only livestock but corn, cloth, honey and apples plus cheese and dairy products. By the 19th century, shipbuilding, brick industries and coalyards were all in full swing. And then of course there were the pubs.

Fives Wall at The Anchor Inn, showing the pub, its sign, and most of the wall

The façade of the Anchor pub hides its origins. From Saxon times until the early 19th century, it is thought that the building was used to conduct the Hundreds Court, with its owners being responsible for the running of the nearby ferry. In the car park is another red-brick Fives Wall, built during the 18th century using local bricks. You may remember that we overlooked a Fives Wall as we descended from Ham Hill to Stoke-sub-Hamdon. For those of you who intend to walk the South Petherton loop, you'll be able to see another Fives Wall.

If we look across the water and a little inland, we'll see what appears to be an old rusty barn. All is not what it seems but I'll come back to that. Standing close to the river just before Combwich Common if we take a line across the river and follow this to the barn, this was the route of the Saxon ferry that was still in use during the very early part of the 20th century. It connected at the far side of the river to a trackway formerly known as the White House Passage. Where *we* are standing on our side of the river, we're at the beginning of another route known as a Herepath. This travels to Cannington Hill Fort, the Quantocks and beyond. Herepaths were the Saxon equivalent of the Roman Fosse Way and Ermine Street, the latter today's A1. All were constructed as military routes for the movement of soldiers.

And now to the unveiling of the old, rusty barn. This corrugated construction is in fact a Second World War RAF Barrage Balloon hanger. These huge balloons were sixty-six feet long and thirty feet high and acted as a deterrent to prevent low flying aircraft and pinpoint bombing by the Luftwaffe.

As we walked beside the Bridgwater and Taunton canal, we passed several pillboxes, all part of the South Coast Stop Line. Here, as we overlook Pawlett Hams and Pawlett village we're viewing a Site of Special Interest relating to military defences which includes the balloon hanger. At Puriton, approximately three miles beyond Pawlett, is an ammunition factory constructed during the early days of the war. Requiring millions of gallons of water, it was fed by the artificially-dug Huntspill River, again created during the war. Designed by the Royal Ordnance Factory to produce explosives, the factory must have been a prime target for enemy aircraft.

If we continue on that theme think of the line of the River Parrett, the line of the Bridgwater and Taunton canal plus the nearby Bristol to Taunton railway line. What lies at Taunton? The United Kingdom Hydrographic Office, another prime target made easier by these navigational aids.

River Parrett at low tide, Combwich

Steart Marshes, now a Nature Reserve, was created as a natural barrier to newly-built flood banks. This area will be sheer heaven for those of you who love flora and fauna. Here you'll find purple loosestrife and flowering rushes. Salt lamb and beef cattle are reared here too. Just enjoy being here, enjoy the great outdoors. As you walk the trail you'll be walking more or less parallel to the narrow road which leads to the tiny village of Steart.

I think it's about time to explain names again. Steart, once spelt 'Stert' as in Stert Point, is derived from an Old English name *steort* meaning a projecting piece of land. Two such similar names close to each other does seem strange. Would this have evolved because of mispronunciation by those speaking the local dialect? This tiny village lies within the Bridgwater Bay area, and during the Second World War was all part of a secret MI6 organisation. Called The Radio Security Service, it used to locate and interpret messages sent by their counterparts, the German Secret Intelligence Service. It is difficult now to think just how important this tiny village was during the conflict.

This is where my excitement always begins when walking this trail, now that we're so close to our goal of Stert Point.

However, just before we reach this point, we'll arrive at a tiny car park, where we'll discover there are other walks that start from here. So, if you've enjoyed this 50 mile trek, why not consider walking these other trails – the West Somerset Coast Path, which is 58 miles and then, a really big challenge, the newly linked England Coast Path of approximately 3,000 miles. Wow!

As we take our last few steps, we'll pass a tranquil pond where bullrushes grow, a chicken farm, and some delightful homes. It's an easy walk of approximately a mile. And now, here we are at our final goal, the bird hide.

Weather permitting, we'll see spectacular views: to the north, Steepholm, Flatholm and Wales, and Burnham-on-Sea with its famous red and white striped lighthouse. To the east, on a clear day you can see the Mendip transmitter and Puriton. To the west and across the sea are the chimneys of Newport, South Wales, and to the south, the eastern end of the Quantock Hills.

More to the point, keep looking south and imagining the Dorset Hills 50 miles away where we started this wonderful trek, and where the Parrett started its life in the reedbeds at Chedington. After we'd passed through North Perrott, we reached the ruins of an old grist mill where the river had already grown in width. Approaching Kingsbury Episcopi church, the river was now in its teenage stage. And now here at Stert Point we see it as a fully grown up and mighty River Parrett, which at its widest, is 700 yards from bank to bank.

It is spectacular! In my words, just amazing!

Whether you have read, or walked and read, hopefully you'll have made discoveries – in itself a great achievement!

So, there's only one thing left to do – celebrate!

Postscript

Having read my jottings, hopefully when you next travel to new areas of the country you'll look at the landscapes and think 'let me discover the industries that have been created here, where I'm standing'.

Places you may think of are Derbyshire, which in the main is carboniferous limestone and millstone grit, Dartmoor granite and within it, tin, copper, silver and lead.

Move to Cornwall and the majority of its rock is brown marine sandstone.

A little nearer to Somerset is the Isle of Portland in Dorset, created by a capping of limestone, used to build St Paul's Cathedral.

Discover the industries that all these formations have created and why. Perhaps you too will have this irresistible feeling that you want and need to understand a little more of our amazing geology. To understand is to see!

Sections of the route with their geological units and ages*

Chapter 1, Chedington to Merriott,
10.5k (6.55ml) **page 6**

107 million years ago
The Chalk	Upper Cretaceous Chalk
Upper Greensand (UGS)	Mid-Cretaceous sand and sandstone

167 million years ago
Forest Marble	Middle Jurassic marls and limestone
Frome Clay	Middle Jurassic marls
Fullers Earth	Middle Jurassic marls
Inferior Oolite	Middle Jurassic limestone

174 million years ago
Bridport Sand	Lower Jurassic sand and sandstone

Chapter 2, Merriott to Ham Hill,
10m (6.25ml) **page 15**

167 million years ago
Forest Marble	Middle Jurassic marls and limestone
Frome Clay	Middle Jurassic marls
Fullers Earth	Middle Jurassic marls
Inferior Oolite	Middle Jurassic limestone
Bridport Sand (inc. Ham Stone)	Lower Jurassic sand and sandstone
Beacon Limestone (Junction Bed)	Lower Jurassic limestone

175 million years ago
Dyrham Formation	Lower Jurassic sands, silts and mudstones

Chapter 3, Ham Hill
page 21

167 million years ago
Bridport Sand (inc. Ham Stone)	Lower Jurassic sand and sandstone

* The Periods above are given as average time-scales

Grid references

The following references are a general guide to the line of the route highlighting places seen and walked through. Explorer Maps 117, 128*, 129** and 140 are all within Ordnance Survey **ST** grid references. Explorer Map 116 is within Ordnance Survey **SY** grid references

Place	Map	Grid Ref.
Chedington	116/117	490590
South Perrott	"	062477
North Perrott	"	475095
Haselbury Mill	129	460115
Merriott Lock Up	"	446125
Lower Stratton	"	444152
Norton-sub-Hamdon	"	471158
Ham Hill War Memorial	"	477173
Bower Hinton	"	459180
Parrett Works	"	446187
East Lambrook (brook)	"	437188
Kingsbury Episcopi	"	434210
Thorney Bridge	"	427229
Muchelney Westover Bridge	"	425248
Langport Huish Bridge	"	424263
Stathe Bridge	140	375291
Burrow Mump	"	359305
Westonzoyland Pumping Station	"	339328
Fordgate, Bridgwater and Taunton Canal	"	322326
Bridgwater Docks	"	299375
Dunball Wharf	"	308409
Combwich	"	260424
Steart Drove, Steart Marshes Nature Reserve	"	261450
Dowells Farm car park	"	275459
Bird hide near Stert Point	"	282468

* Map 128 and 140 show the alternative route from Stathe via Stoke St Gregory to Burrowbridge and Burrow Mump.

** Map 129 shows the alternative route from Lower Stratton via South Petherton to East Lambrook.

Table of Geological Units and their ages

*Those in **Bold** are crossed or seen from the Parrett Trail*

Era	Period	MYA	Duration
Cenozoic	Quaternary	2.6-0	2.6
	Neogene	23-2.6	20.4
	Paleogene	66-23	43
Mesozoic	**Cretaceous**	**145-66**	**79**
	Jurassic	**201-145**	**56**
	Triassic	**252-201**	**51**
Palaeozoic	Permian	299-252	47
	Carboniferous	359-299	60
	Devonian	**419-359**	**60 = Quantock Hills**
	Silurian	444-419	25
	Ordovician	485-444	41
	Cambrian	541-485	56

MYA = Millions of years ago
Duration = Millions of years per period